Neil Leatherbarrow is a first-time author and founder and CEO of the Charlotte Leatherbarrow Foundation, which has been active since July 2011. Before this he was a musician with the band No Longer Music. He then went on to manage youth work and gap year teams for fifteen years, working for different church mission and local government agencies, both here in the UK and across Europe.

# All That You
# Can Leave Behind

NEIL LEATHERBARROW

# All That You Can
# Leave Behind

**Pegasus**

PEGASUS PAPERBACK

© Copyright 2015
**Neil Leatherbarrow**

The right of Neil Leatherbarrow to be identified as author of
this work has been asserted by him in accordance with the
Copyright, Designs and Patents Act 1988

A CIP catalogue record for this title is
available from the British Library

ISBN: 9781903490891

Permission has been granted by David Edwards for the lyrics to his song,
'Dancing like the Angels'.

Permission has been granted by Dr Tony Campolo's sermon,
'It's Friday, but Sunday's coming'.

Scripture taken from the HOLY BIBLE, NEW INTERNATIONAL VERSION*.
Copyright © 1973, 1978, 1984 by International Bible Society.
Used by permission of Zondervan Publishing House. All rights reserved.

*Pegasus is an imprint of*
*Pegasus Elliot Mackenzie Publishers Ltd.*
www.pegasuspublishers.com

**First Published in 2015**

**Pegasus**
**Sheraton House Castle Park**
**Cambridge CB3 0AX England**

Printed & Bound in Great Britain

*To Charlotte — I will never forget you.*

# Acknowledgements

To my wife, Karen, and my sons, Luke and Jason, and to all my friends who have walked with me on this my hardest journey.

# Introduction
## War on Grief

I am writing this book to give an honest and real account of what happened. I'm not pretending to be an expert on how to handle grief. I am just a casualty of war. This is the personal journey of someone who is in the trenches of grief, still trying to find the courage to go over the top into no man's land, ducking for cover when the enemy's forces are overwhelming, waiting for the reinforcement of hope to show me the way and searching for the strength to carry on fighting another day.

I can only imagine what a real war is like as I am not a soldier. But from the day I lost my twelve-year-old daughter, I declared war on grief, determined not to be beaten by it or allow it to tear apart what was left of my family. The grief of losing a child feels like entering into a fight when you already know your opponent will win. My grief knocks me down time and time again. For me, to win is to keep trying to get back up again. Grief is inevitable. How I deal with it will determine what kind of future I will have. Denial would cause more pain. Facing it will still be painful and yet offer an alternative.

Looking back on my childhood, the challenges and the scars would grant me strength to face a long hard road ahead.

Grief can be an extremely destructive force. Statistically, nine out of ten marriages end in divorce and the surviving children feel they lose their parents as well. I could try to justify why this tragedy happened and blame others for my loss, but this would lead to further pain and brokenness.

There are stages in grief, or so I'm told. But there is no logic, no order in my grief. I am surrounded by an enemy that attacks me at random. Like my daughter's fatal collision with a bus, there is no scientific or theological reason to explain how or why she died. Her life was left to random chance. I'm fighting a private war. I have to accept and acknowledge that even within my own family we grieve in different ways.

At times my pain throws my mind into turmoil and every truth I have ever believed in is turned inside-out, exposed by my grief. In this unholy war I am stripped bare, vulnerable and naked. My emotions are left feeling raw and tender. This is my ultimate test in life. This is where my faith will make a last stand and this is where my story begins...

# Chapter 1
## Shock Wave

It was Thursday, March 17, 2011. I had just finished teaching a bunch of international students on post-modern youth culture in Karlsruhe, Germany, and was sitting in my guest room with my laptop, trying to Skype my wife Karen and the kids back home. There was no answer so I thought I'd leave it for a while and try again later. I knew that Karen was probably rushing Charlotte to get her to the local dance school on time. At around seven o'clock I noticed a missed call from Karen on my mobile phone and then, just as I was about to phone, I received a call from her. Her voice was clearly shaken and very upset.

"Neil, you need to come home – there's been a terrible accident!"

My immediate thought was that Karen had been involved in a car accident. I remained calm and asked, "Are you alright?"

Karen replied, sounding more frantic, "Neil, you need to come home now. It's Charlotte. She's been hit by a bus!"

"Why — what happened?"

"Do you really want me to tell you over the phone?!"

"Yes."

"She's dead, she's dead… she's dead, Neil. Just come home now!" Karen's voice broke down, sobbing uncontrollably.

I was dumbfounded and struggled to find any words to say.

"Okay… I'm coming home, sweetheart… I'm going to catch the last flight out of Germany. I'll call you later…"

A sudden shockwave struck me. I leaned against the wall of my room to stop myself from falling over. In fact, it felt more like a tidal wave and from this moment on I was in perpetual shock. I had to gather my thoughts quickly and concentrate on getting home as fast as possible. My time spent trying to get home that night was frustrating beyond belief. I was told I could get a standby ticket on the last flight out of Germany.

I arrived at the airport with twenty minutes to spare and ran to the flight desk to buy my ticket home. My voice sounded desperate as I quickly explained to the desk clerk what was happening back home. She just sat there staring back at me, expressionless, and told me I was too late to buy a ticket and board the plane. My eyes widened. I couldn't believe how this woman was treating me with such indifference. I broke down crying and pleaded with her to let me on the plane. She picked up the phone and, after a brief discussion with someone, hung up. She looked straight into my bloodshot eyes and with a cold voice informed me there was nothing she could do. I left the airport dumbfounded. I had been indiscriminately tossed to one side like a piece of dirt; my daughter's death meant absolutely nothing to them.

I had to phone Karen and tell her I wasn't coming home that night. She was still at the scene of the fatal collision where the police had sealed off the road. The area had now become a crash investigation site. The paramedics had covered Charlotte's body where she was still lying under the bus. Thank God my dear and faithful friends Paul and Heidi were there to comfort Karen and my boys, Luke and Jason. Karen described to me how she was driving Charlotte to her dance class and the traffic was piled up on Herne Hill. So, she let her out to cross the road and when she ran, she was hit by a double-decker bus. Jason, our fourteen-year-old son, was sitting in the back of the car and witnessed the collision. Karen told me how brave he was that night, holding her tightly, his first words were of comfort, "It's okay, Mummy. Charlotte is with Jesus now."

I so badly wanted to be with them and felt so completely frustrated that I was not. There was a crushing pain in my heart that seemed to dull my anger. I told Karen I would call her again to let her know when I had booked the first flight out of Germany in the morning. When I hung up and was on my way back to the guesthouse, I cried out, "My baby's gone, my baby's gone!" My heart was broken.

I retired to my room exhausted. I tossed and turned all night, wrestling with my thoughts. I searched the night sky out of my window, looking for some kind of sign that everything was going to be all right. I was overcome with despair and felt lost in a sea of emotion. That was probably the loneliest night I had spent in my entire life. The roads were empty traveling to Frankfurt airport in the early hours of the morning. There was an eerie silence, and I don't know if it was just exhaustion or that I genuinely felt more at peace. It was as if God had given me some sort of reassurance that Charlotte was safe in His arms. Whatever it was, I had the strength to face my darkest hour. The journey home seemed endless and the relief was immense when I made my way out of London City Airport that morning.

The reality of losing Charlotte hit me more when I saw my friends at arrivals. The shock on their faces said it all. How could this have happened? By the time we reached my home, I was shaking like a leaf. I paused for a moment standing outside the front door and thought to myself – life will never be the same for my family. Whatever was meant to be before Charlotte's death was now being rewritten. The future looked very uncertain. I had woken up that morning to an alternate reality and now, walking through this door, I was going to realize my worst nightmare.

I wasn't prepared. How could you be prepared for something like this? I felt weak, vulnerable, scared and angry all at the same time. I hadn't felt like this since I was a boy. My mind flashed back to when I walked into our lounge one night and found a strange man lying naked on top of my mother. It was a complete shock. I surprised myself with the kind of language that came out of my mouth and the stranger's violent reaction towards me. This strange intruder was later to become my first stepfather. That night I did a lot of growing up with the shocking realization that the world I lived in wasn't safe at all. I was nine years old.

I felt like that boy again as I stood in my front doorway. All the tough lessons I had learnt growing up, all the stupid things I had ever done. I was a juvenile delinquent in a street gang, breaking and entering, stealing, and joyriding in stolen cars. I didn't know or care if I was going to live or die. I was used to fighting with fists, with knives, on probation, drunk and so high I couldn't remember how I rode home safely on my motorbike.

Then at the age of sixteen, I turned my life around, following a truth and a way of life that was so alien to me and yet changed my private world. I had lived my life daring to do things some would not consider. I had seen some amazing things happen. But probably the most life-changing thing I had ever done was to get married to a woman who fitted me perfectly like a well-tailored glove. Together we raised three beautiful children and I was determined not to repeat the history of my own childhood but to change it by pouring my heart and soul into loving my family with everything I had to give.

Through all these things, I always felt I would be prepared for whatever life had to throw at me. Except for this – losing my daughter. I was still nauseous with shock. My world didn't feel safe again and was about to take a turn for the worse as I opened my front door.

I had been married to Karen for twenty-one years; we were soul mates. Nothing and nobody had ever tested our relationship like this before. Karen is a strong and compassionate woman and trained as a nurse at St. Thomas's hospital in London. When we were first married I would pick her up in our car after she completed a night shift, her uniform often covered in blood. She would excitedly tell me all about her night of drama in casualty, such as how a man had thrown himself in front of a tube train and severed his arm yet miraculously survived the ordeal.

Another time, Karen and I were walking by the river Thames with some friends on a nice Sunday afternoon. We were passing a building site with one of those industrial cranes, at least one hundred feet tall, and a high fence around the whole site. All of a sudden we heard what could only be described as someone's blood-curdling scream silenced as they hit the concrete inside the fenced area. Before I could say anything, Karen was running to find the entrance to get into the building site.

I chased after her and by the time I had caught up, she was kneeling down beside what looked like a dead body. As I drew closer I saw one of the most horrific scenes I have ever witnessed. A man lying face down on concrete, his arms and legs twisted and bent. His head was cracked open in a pool of blood. Half of his face and brains was scattered around his body. Karen was in super nurse mode, one hand on his neck feeling for a pulse and the other on her mobile to the emergency services. They wanted her to turn the body over to try and get his heart going. I glared at her and told her firmly there was no way we were going to turn him over.

I shuddered at the thought of what we might see. I had already trodden on part of his face or brain. I certainly didn't want to see what was left. I told Karen they must be joking if they thought she could try to revive him. Fortunately, by this time the police and paramedics arrived and took control of the situation. This was a shocking scene to witness and one that Karen and I talked about for weeks afterwards. As traumatic as this was, and what looked like a suicide, Karen was able to cope with this kind of tragic incident as she was trained for it. As a nurse she had engaged in so many of life's dramas.

But this was so different for her now, a mother witnessing her own daughter's horrific death. I will never forget how fragile she was that day, the tortured look on her face, her eyes full of despair as we held each other for a long time. She was tormented with regret for letting Charlotte out of the car. I reassured her that we were going to get through this together, that we would not let this destroy our family. Unless the bus driver was found guilty of negligence, this was an accident. I wasn't going to blame her. Everyone makes mistakes crossing a road and most of the time we escape injury and certain death.

I told her our love for each other, our boys, and what was left of our battered faith was going to hold us together. If Karen and I had a mission in life, it was to "love your neighbour as yourself". After living this out for so long it becomes a part of your DNA, a second nature. Even though we were tempted to run for the hills or hide under the bed covers, shutting out the world around us, we felt compelled to open our home and our hearts to all our friends and family who wanted to come and grieve with us.

This choice took us by surprise. We hadn't realized how many people Charlotte had reached. We must have had at least a hundred people pass through our door during the first week after Charlotte's death. Her influence was larger than we thought and so many friends wanted to show their support. There were over four hundred cards of condolence and our kitchen and lounge looked like a florist's dream. We were given so many meals we not only filled our own freezer but our neighbour's too. I don't know why, but it's often the worst circumstances that bring out the best in us.

Charlotte was a young performer, a dancer, and already by the age of eleven had accumulated a string of achievements to her name. In September 2010 she auditioned for a role in the West End show *Billy Elliot*. By the end of a month's hard work she landed a part as one of the Ballet Girls. She was the youngest performer to have played Sharon Percy. Charlotte was twelve years old and four months into the show when her life was cut short. There were seventy-five Google pages dedicated to Charlotte's story. They varied from the national newspapers reporting 'bus crash horror for young *Billy Elliot* star' to Perez Hilton, Hollywood's most popular celebrity gossip and blogger.

I remember going online and looking at the comments made on Perez's blog. Most of them were sympathetic, but there were those that just said something like, 'I hope it's not the case that this girl wanted to cross without a green man and a bus driver driving like normal was the unfortunate victim of the situation', and 'Her parents should have taught her to ALWAYS look both ways before crossing the street'.

These comments were so raw and harsh for a grieving father to read. It amazes me when someone can be so removed from the reality of what we were going through and yet still to be so flippant, so judgmental at a time when we were so vulnerable. This was so cruel.

On Wednesday, March 23, Karen and I were finally going to see our daughter. I had been frustrated with the lack of communication between our family liaison officer and the

22

Coroner's Office at Greenwich. The liaison officer advised me not to see Charlotte until she was taken to the funeral home because of the damage to her head and face. But if I wanted to, I could go to the mortuary at any time. Unfortunately, Charlotte had been taken to Greenwich mortuary on the night of the accident. Greenwich was where the 'on call' coroner came from, even though there was a mortuary at King's College Hospital just down the road from where we lived.

I anxiously wanted to see Charlotte. In my state of shock I needed to see proof of her death. When I phoned the Coroner's Office they informed me they needed permission from the liaison officer before I was allowed to see my daughter. Frustrated, I tried phoning the liaison officer during that first week with no success. The coroner also took longer than usual to perform his autopsy, and, because I had no permission, I wasn't allowed to see Charlotte. Only when she had been moved to the funeral home of our choice did we finally get to see her.

It had almost been a week and neither of us had slept well. Karen was inconsolable, crying herself to sleep and waking up distraught in the mornings. She had taken Charlotte's two little teddies, Heartsweet and Stitch, and wrapped them in her 'I love snoozing' nighty, placing them between us in our bed. I had been plagued by violent thoughts and nightmares. My imagination was running riot with how Charlotte's fatal collision happened. There was a physical ache in my heart and I wanted to feel close to Charlotte. We sat in the reception of the funeral home waiting for the funeral director to come and show us to the room where Charlotte was resting.

I thought back to last Wednesday. I was sitting in a restaurant at Stansted Airport's departure lounge eating a hamburger and talking to Charlotte on my mobile. She was telling me, enthusiastically, how she had single-handedly pulled out her baby eye tooth. She was pleased to hear me tell her that her front teeth had room to straighten out now. She was in a rush, as usual, to get out the door and go to her dance lesson. I told her I loved her and said goodbye. That was the last time I spoke to Charlotte.

Karen had brought the photos of Charlotte taken in a professional studio. She had a feeling we might need them. The director walked in looking apprehensive and asked if we were ready. She was kind and sympathetic as she explained the funeral arrangements to us. Her partner was the coroner on call that night so she was aware of how Charlotte had died. The Co-op funeral care would not charge us for anything because Charlotte was a child. It was very compassionate of them to do so. Karen showed her the photos. She looked puzzled and asked, "Is this your daughter?"

She didn't recognize the girl in the photos. Her eyes welled up with tears as she turned and pleaded with us not to see her lying in the coffin. She wanted us to remember her as she was in these photographs. Nevertheless, we insisted on seeing her so she led us out to the back where Charlotte lay. As she opened the door I could see the room was dimly lit, and the coffin was at the other end. Before we went in she told us they had done their very best to wax Charlotte's face to keep it together. We were warned not to touch anything due to the extent of her injuries, or her face and head would fall apart.

Karen walked in first, took a quick look, and then turned her head away from the coffin. I followed in trepidation and walked right up to the coffin. I had imagined this moment and romanticized that Charlotte would somehow look angelic. She was wearing the beautiful white dress we had bought her a few days earlier. The funeral director had covered up her chest where the pathologist had cut her open for the autopsy. Charlotte's hands were already discolored, her fingers stiff with rigor mortis.

I stared long and hard into Charlotte's inert face. Her last moments on this earth did not look like they had been peaceful at all. She had the look of someone who had just seen a ghost. Her teeth were yellow, her head and face misshapen. Her eyes wide open, sunken and lifeless. I grabbed the side of the coffin. I desperately wanted to hold and kiss my daughter, to tell her that everything was okay now. I wanted to reassure her that she was in a safe place where there was no more pain, no more suffering. Instead I was speechless and felt like someone had just cut my chest open and ripped my heart out.

I collapsed into the chair beside her. I could only feel death in this room, no life. It was choking me and I had to get out. There was nothing angelic about seeing my dead daughter's body. What I had experienced was more like taking communion with the devil and he was laughing in my face. What I saw that day was an empty shell. Charlotte's soul had departed and my daughter that I cherished and loved so dearly... was gone.

# Chapter 2
## A Rude Awakening

Looking back over my shoulder, the 1970s seemed a depressing era. We had the industrial unrest of the miners' strikes, national power cuts, and high unemployment. 1975 was a particularly turbulent year, not that I was so aware of what was going on in the world around me, but life at home took a turn for the worse. I had been living in Bridgend, Wales, for a year and just returned for my first year at junior school in September. My mother came to collect me before my first day had even started. She made the excuse that my grandmother was very ill and we needed to go and visit her. She lived in Chelmsford, Essex, on the other side of the country.

I never returned to Wales because that was the day my mother separated from my father. My older brother, Lance, went to live with my father who had moved back up north to St. Helen's, Lancashire, where he was born and bred. My dad visited me just once that year. He took me to London for the day where we visited the HMS Belfast, the Navy's monument to World War II, and we watched *Jaws* at the movies. It scared the living daylights out of me and my dad couldn't believe it was rated an 'A' (the equivalent of a PG or 12A). I didn't want to go back in the bath, never mind the sea. That was the last time I saw my dad for well over a year.

My mother and I were living with my grandparents. Occasionally we would go over to my uncle and auntie's house for the weekend. I enjoyed hanging out with my cousins and my mum enjoyed the company of her sister's friends. Even though my mum always confided in me a lot about her relationship with my dad, naturally, I was still very naive about sexual relationships. So when I woke up in the middle of the night hearing strange noises coming from underneath my bedroom, I inquisitively stumbled downstairs. I opened the lounge door to find a stranger lying naked on top of my mother.

Immediately I burst into a rage and commanded the stranger to get off my mother or I would kill him. The stranger stood up and I lunged at him, kicking and punching as hard as I could. The grown man shrugged me off like a feather and, in his anger, decided to teach me a lesson I would never forget. This intruder controlled my hysterical behavior by slapping me and then knocking me from one side of the room to the other. I picked myself up from the floor, stunned by the blunt force that put me down, and ran upstairs feeling humiliated. My mother could only look down in shame and embarrassment.

When I woke the next morning, I remembered staring outside of the window thinking, 'This is it, this is as good as it gets'. I felt like I had come of age and become a man overnight. I experienced thoughts and emotions that I'd never felt before. It was then that I realized the world did not revolve around me. For the first time in my life I stared into

27

the future and felt hopelessness. Somehow I knew that my first violent encounter with this stranger was not going to be the last and, to top it all, my mother had fallen in love with this man. I felt very alone, like I had lost someone so important to me and she had betrayed my trust.

After my crude introduction to my future stepfather, my mother and I moved out of my grandparents' house and into a single berth caravan situated in a village just outside of Southend-on-Sea, Essex. Michael was a truck driver whose personal motto in life could be summed up in four words: 'wine, women and song'. He was a rugged-looking man with tattoos on both forearms, a character that was rough, unrefined, and unintelligent. He always had a cigarette in his mouth and a story to tell. Michael had two teenaged children of his own who lived with his ex-wife, while he lived with us virtually all the time.

I slept in one bed while Michael and my mother slept in the other a few feet away from mine. They were still in the beginning of their relationship so sex was a regular event. Naturally, I couldn't sleep and shouted at them to get out of my bedroom. Michael's response was swift in dishing out the physical discipline. A quick swipe of his hand across my face was his usual way of ending an argument. After a fierce exchange of carnal knowledge, I was bullied into submission and all because I was upsetting my mother too much. This episode became too repetitive so I decided it was better not to come home at night. I chose to wander the streets of Hullbridge and look for some action of my own.

I would meet up with some of my friends from the local junior school and here began my life of petty crime, throwing bricks through shop windows, smashing the streetlights, stealing from the supermarket, breaking into cars and generally wreaking havoc on the local neighbourhood. I would be clobbered for returning home late and for worrying my mother. But I didn't care; it was worth it. There was anger, real anger, welling up inside me. It felt like a smouldering volcano, unstoppable, uncontrollable, looking for release. This life of crime was my way out, living on the edge, unpredictable, not knowing what was going to happen next. The adrenaline surge was too exciting to give up.

The local newspaper reported on our extra curricular activities. The police were chasing ghosts and we relished the notoriety. Throughout our two years of crime, we managed to evade capture apart from being caught for truancy from school. What a hypocrite I was turning into, rebelling against the abuse committed against me by abusing other people's property, and yet I seemed hell-bent on this dark path. After a year of living in the caravan together, Michael's mother died and left her two bedroom council house to him.

I thought I could breathe a sigh of relief, finally having my own bedroom. This was short-lived when my seventeen year-old step-brother moved in. He was crazy like his father, an athletic build with bleached blond hair, a Billy Idol look-alike, but I liked Kevin. He introduced me to air rifles and showed me where the old man kept his porn magazines. Both were welcome entertainment, particularly the air rifle. I would use the next-door neighbour's washing, hanging on the line, as target practice.

Then Michael decided to take me under his wing and teach me how to become a real man. He told me I was taking two days off school to go with him on a road trip to Wales and back. Taking time off school I didn't mind but having to spend it with him - I protested profusely. My protest was in vain. Early the next morning we set off for my boy-to-man trip and it did prove to be memorable in more ways than one. First, we stopped at a greasy spoon, full of Michael's truck-driving mates and, like a hungry wolf, I devoured my fried breakfast. Afterwards, Michael gave me a sharp clip round the ear for embarrassing him in front of his mates.

Next we picked up a couple of young girls wearing mini-skirts and lots of make-up, hitching for a lift. Of course Michael was very obliging. He was flirty and put on his usual charm of telling funny stories and cracking jokes. The girls, who couldn't have been much older than eighteen, laughed along. I didn't know if they were just stupid or naive. Maybe they felt safe because I was sitting in the cab with them. We stopped at a service station to eat and tank up. Michael disappeared with the girls for a short time and came back without them, looking flushed in the face. He gave me a look like the cat had just caught the cream.

He told me that now we both shared his dirty little secret, a secret that would hurt me if I ever told my mother what he had done. I looked him straight in the eyes and gave him a filthy look. If he could, I'm sure he would have slapped me, but not in the service station. This was like experiencing a story straight out of one of his porn magazines. Except, this story wasn't funny or thrilling to look at. In fact, I felt dirty, as though I was the one who had betrayed my mother.

Even though I was intimidated and wouldn't dare tell on him, I decided to use his dirty little secret as ammunition against him later on to help convince my mum to leave him for good. I mirrored his devilish grin and thought if only he knew what I was up to with my gang. How I would love to embarrass him if I was ever caught by the police and my criminal life was made public. How the shame of it would bruise his pride.

The only other memory I had of this road trip was on the way back from Wales around three in the morning. Michael let me drive the empty tanker down the M4 while he had a snooze. The road was bare, I was only eleven years old, and my feet could scarcely touch the pedals. The steering wheel was nearly as big as me and I could just about see over the dashboard. The steering only needed a nudge to the left or right and the tanker would swerve in that direction. I had to really concentrate just to keep it in a straight line. But I'll never forget that feeling of power and freedom driving down the motorway doing nearly seventy miles an hour. Michael liked to break the rules and so did I. Maybe this was the only thing we would ever have in common.

There were thoughts I was contemplating that I did not fully understand. The fantasies that porn conjured up in my mind seemed harmless and fun. In reality, seeing my stepfather act them out made me feel dirty. Then there was the anger and vengeance I felt towards Michael and the injustice I was causing my neighbours. I was changing, a rebel with a cause. There was a poison inside, running through my veins that was corrupting me. The more I hated Michael, the more I became like him. Was there any escape?

1977 was a good year in many ways. If my memory serves me correctly, my football team, Hullbridge Sports, were runners-up in the league. I collected a medal and shook hands with Peter Taylor, who played for Tottenham Hotspur. This was a very proud moment for me, shaking hands with a famous footballer. Our school had its first overseas trip, to Belgium, where we each bought a Mannekin Pis corkscrew, much to our amusement. This is a famous Brussels landmark where a small bronze fountain sculpture depicts a naked little Dutch boy urinating into the fountain's basin.

We all watched Liverpool FC beat Borussia Monchengladbach 3-1 in the European Cup Final. I can remember walking into a school hall where the game was televised live and projected onto a big screen at the front. Our Belgian hosts and their school children were all chanting in their seats, "Liverpool, ha ha ha!"

My teachers glared at my friends and me just to make sure we didn't start a riot in the middle of the hall. By the end of the game we had the last laugh, and it was our turn to taunt them, "Borussia, ha ha ha!"

It was also the Queen's Silver Jubilee Birthday and we celebrated with a street party. I dressed up as a one-man band, all in Union Jack colours, and won the fancy dress competition. I had the Union Jack painted on my face and the outfit I was wearing was so tight I almost passed out. The big bass drum on my back was heavy too. I guess it was worth it just to win, although I can't even remember what the prize was. I think my mum wanted to win more than I did. My mother, Pauline Ann, was a pretty woman with dark hair and stunning blue-green eyes. She had a sporty looking figure and her nickname was Spitfire Annie. She was known for her quick temper and sharp tongue that could reduce any grown man to tears.

Since she had been with Michael, my mum had resigned herself to work in a factory for Wranglers Jeans instead of her normal job as a primary school teacher. She was thirty-eight years old in 1977 and time was creeping up on her. The lines on her face drew a picture of stress and pain. I didn't know why she tolerated Michael's philandering. Half of the time she had a permanent glaze in her eyes and slept through the drama going on around her. When my mum was *compos mentis* and coherent we would plot our escape from the nightmare on Abbey Road. But every time we actually came to leaving, my mother would change her mind, as if Michael had cast a spell over her.

During the summer break I was able to visit my dad and brother for a couple of weeks. This was the first time I'd seen them since the winter of 1975. They had moved to a place called Minehead in Somerset. My brother, Lance, had become asthmatic living in St. Helens, so my dad decided to move out to the country to improve his health. Lance was two years older than me, skinny and a little taller. He was a handsome-looking teenager with deep dark-brown eyes and a mop of dark-brown hair. We shared a lot of common likes and dislikes in movies and music.

Minehead was a sleepy seaside town dominated in the summer by Butlin's holiday campers. With the beach on one side and the beautiful Exmoor country on the other, Minehead was a perfect place to escape from the troubles of life. This was also my chance to see the long-awaited sci-fi blockbuster *Star Wars*. It had been released in London at the beginning of the year but didn't reach the shores of Minehead until the summer.

The local flea pit, the Regal Cinema, was screening it. The cinema was still fitted with mono sound. The owner literally ran around doing everything from selling the tickets and running the projector, to serving ice cream during the intermission. Tickets cost just fifty pence, which was a bargain even for those days. My brother and I went to see the movie every night for two weeks. Most of the time we were the only customers, but did we care?

Star Wars, A New Hope, the Force, the Empire, the Rebellion, 'Help me Obi-Wan Kenobi, you're my only hope', and it was all happening in a galaxy far, far away. I was lost in a fantasy world of complete escapism. Finally I could lose myself, forget about the depressing reality of my life and become the hero I always wanted to be, Luke Skywalker. *Star Wars* had taken the world by storm and, in a world where there was high unemployment, *Star Wars* gave everyone hope. At least it gave me a break for a couple of hours.

Meanwhile, back in Abbey Road, a storm was looming over my home. Michael's moods grew darker and his behaviour more aggressive. That year I had already called 999 twice for the ambulance to come around. Once it was because my mum was bleeding so badly, the other time was for her overdosing on a drug. Valium is an addictive sedative which she had been taking for many years. I was also called out of school once when my mum had collapsed at a bus stop and was rushed to hospital.

By the time the summer of 1978 had arrived, my relationship with Michael had completely broken down.

During many confrontations we threatened to kill each other. Sometimes in the middle of the night I would wake up with a fright and see Michael standing over me, menacingly, holding a weapon. Other times he would just wake me to belt me across the face and remind me who was the boss in his house. His tactics worked. I felt very intimidated and this would be an enduring image, a splinter in my mind's eye that haunted me for the rest of my life.

However, I felt I had gained a small victory in the violent struggle against my stepfather. He had a lock fitted on the outside of my bedroom door, ironically to make sure I didn't disturb or attack him in the night. I distinctly remember one time when Michael came home from a party inebriated and locked my mother in the lounge. First came the profanities and then the fists. I tried to break the door down with no success. I felt helpless so I shouted at the door, calling Michael every name under the sun. The door burst open and he started to pound on me. Michael was crafty. He wouldn't clench his fists but instead he cupped his hands, slapping me hard across the face with enough force to knock me to the floor.

I took the fight into the kitchen where I grabbed a knife from one of the drawers and tried to stick it right in his heart. But he was too strong and forced the knife out of my hand. He knocked me down several times until I stopped trying to get back up because my head was too sore, and I felt very dizzy. He then proceeded back into the lounge and started to beat my mother again. He had done this before but that night was different. He sounded like he wasn't going to stop.

I panicked and phoned my Uncle Graham, who lived at the other end of Hullbridge. I told him what was happening and pleaded with him to come and save my mother. He drove straight around in his car. Fortunately my uncle was a big man, cool, calm and collected. I don't remember how, but he managed to stop Michael from beating my mother any further. After that night, my mum, demoralized and defeated, told me she was finally ready to leave Michael for good. I felt traumatized from the fight and victorious at the same time. I had finally convinced my mum to leave Michael.

I spent the summer break visiting my dad and brother again. This time I didn't want the holiday to end. I had nightmares about Michael. I had crossed some kind of boundary. I actually tried to kill a man. There were murderous thoughts going through my head. A knot began to tighten in my stomach telling me that all was not well at home. Lance had decided to come back to Hullbridge with me. He hadn't seen our mother for over two years. I was glad for the moral support as I wasn't anticipating a very warm greeting on our return.

Sure enough my intuition served me well; I received a frosty reception from my mother. I tried to reconnect with her and refresh her memory of what we were going to do. But she betrayed my loyalty again and had joined forces with the fork-tongued Michael. Just like an amnesiac, she had forgotten what we had planned together for the last few months. This bad news sickened me to the bone. I'd had enough. I had to get off this rollercoaster ride of emotion and leave this dark place. I had to accept my failure in trying to win my mother over and persuade her to leave Michael.

I could not break this addiction between them; instead I had to look out for my own wellbeing. I sat on my bed, physically shaking and close to tears. I confided in Lance and told him the full story of what had been going on between Michael, our mum and me. My brother tried to reassure me that everything was going to be okay and suggested I phone our dad. I don't know why, but now I felt like the traitor talking with my dad on the phone. I was very guarded in our conversation for fear that Michael or my mum was listening. I asked him to rescue me and take me back with Lance. My dad comforted me as much as he could and said that he would work it out when he came down to pick us up in his car.

All I had to do now was wait... My dad, Alan, was a charismatic-looking figure, five feet ten inches, short black hair, and dark brown eyes. Since the age of fifteen he had been working in journalism, nine of those years in Fleet Street, working as an industrial correspondent. He had cultivated a nice beer belly and dark bags under his eyes. But his good looks and charm could still win the heart of a more impressionable young woman. By this time, he had settled down working as the chief reporter for the local newspaper, *The West Somerset Free Press*. He wasn't the father figure that had abandoned me for almost two years but my hero racing to rescue me from an evil oppressor.

The night when my dad arrived, I was full of fear and anxiety. Both my mother and Michael were unpredictable and I just couldn't gauge how they were going to react. When I sat down with them to announce my departure, the atmosphere in that kitchen could have been cut with a knife.

My mother's face turned pale like a ghost and Michael just put his head down in resignation.

I was free. For the first time I was making my own decisions that would change the course of my life. But my heart felt heavy and my mind was confused. There were so many conflicting thoughts running through my head as I packed my suitcase. I felt free from the cage that Michael held me in and yet heartbroken at the thought of leaving my mother behind. She was vulnerable to Michael's capricious mind and malicious intent.

As we pulled away in the car, I looked across at my mother standing in the doorway. Her face revealed her mortal wound, as if I had committed the unthinkable crime. I had always been there for my mum, her sympathiser, her defender, her rescuer, and now I was deserting her. A wave of despair came over me and I couldn't hold it back any longer. Tears streaming down my face, I sobbed uncontrollably. It had been an intense three years of extreme emotions, thoughts, and experiences that would shape my life for years to come. It had indeed been a rude awakening and yet only the beginning.

# Chapter 3
## Fix It

In January 2008, when Charlotte was just eight years old, she was awake one night with what seemed like a persistent vomiting bug. She was still vomiting the next morning so Karen and I decided to call for an ambulance as she was looking very dehydrated. The A&E staff discovered Charlotte had a burst appendix and informed us she would need keyhole surgery to take the appendix out, an operation around forty-five minutes in duration. Karen and I waited for almost four hours before she came out of surgery.

It's amazing what goes through your mind when faced with a situation like this. We didn't know what was going on and we were left feeling there was nothing we could do except pray. Somehow, though, you tell yourself everything is going to be okay. We had done everything we could by acting swiftly and now Charlotte was in good hands – surely? Of course, in the end I still ended up thinking the worst and then praying for the best.

It turned out that the surgery took so long because the surgeons couldn't find her appendix. It was hiding under her liver. Charlotte was kept in hospital for five days to make sure the infection from her poisoned appendix had cleared up. Karen stayed with her and made sure Charlotte had no fear of being kept in hospital. She played a game where they would rate how kind and handsome the different doctors were who visited her during their daily rounds. There was a huge sigh of relief when she was finally allowed to come home. Charlotte was very brave and kept on smiling and giggling throughout her ordeal.

Throughout life's family dramas I would find a solution to the problem. If something needed to be fixed, there was always a way I could fix it. A ruptured appendix was something beyond my power to mend and so I had to put my trust in the hands of someone else. Those four hours waiting for the outcome of Charlotte's surgery felt more like an eternity and there was nothing I could do. In the same way, with grief, this is where the dilemma only begins.

With Charlotte's sudden death I felt completely helpless and powerless to do anything. I was five hundred miles away when the fatal collision occurred. There was no warning. Charlotte was a sensible girl and had never been involved in an accident before. She was not prone to making mistakes crossing a road. I could not comprehend why she had rushed out in front of an oncoming vehicle, especially a bus. Karen thought she had misunderstood her instruction of when to cross the road. What was going through her mind? There was and is no rational reason to explain why Charlotte was killed.

Every passage of thought I went down led to a dead end – no answer, no solution. This was not meant to happen. But the harsh truth slammed me in the face every time I thought this. My daughter was dead. This unbelievable truth hit me over and over like an unstoppable wave of desperate emotion. All I could do was try and stand up and take it as this overwhelming force struck me.

My beliefs were under attack. I have lived and believed in the power of redemption; everyone deserves a second chance. As a teenager, how many times had I potentially taken my life and others into my own hands, risking it all for nothing? Yet I believed I had been given a second chance to redeem myself and not repeat the mistakes I had made before. Why, when Charlotte had everything going for her, was she not given a second chance? Her death was senseless, meaningless. My thoughts tortured my beliefs.

When Karen and I came out of the funeral home that day, we just wanted to walk off into the horizon and never look back. Our sons were probably the only reason we didn't. Family and friends came around to our house, they hugged, they cried, they made us meals. They helped us plan and organise the inevitable. They visited our house in waves. So did our grief, knocking us out for periods of time during the day, just like an unwelcome visitor in our home trying to find a way to wear us down. This war on grief made us feel nauseous and faint with pain. We had to learn to rest as if we were wounded in battle and then taken off to a medical station to recover.

Our boys had taken time off school. Their friends had come around to comfort them and be a welcome distraction from the chaos that surrounded us. It was the end of March and the Easter break. Luke, our seventeen year-old, was in the middle of studying for his A Level exams coming up in June. Jason was fourteen years old and also studying, preparing for four GCSE exams early in June. The strength of character they both displayed was incredible. How they were able to remain focused on their revision I don't know — but I was so proud of them.

Family time around the dinner table was always a priority for us. No matter how busy the day had been, we always made time to talk. Karen and I encouraged our children to express and articulate themselves, to share what happened and how it made them feel. As they looked back on their day, they all had different stories to tell and learn from each other. They had the freedom to leave no stone unturned and enjoyed the focus of our complete attention.

We had come to a collective decision to cremate Charlotte's body on April 1st, which was a Friday. This needed to be a private ceremony involving close family and friends. A memorial service would follow that Sunday with an invitation extended to everyone who knew Charlotte and our family. At this point I started to feel numb and everything I was doing or saying was disconnected. It was almost as if my brain had switched onto remote control to compensate and divert the pain going on everywhere else.

Organising both services had now become the project from hell. I was forced to fix something I had never in my wildest dreams imagined would break, and I couldn't. Yet, at the same time, I wanted to give my daughter the best send-off any dad could give. It was invaluable to have friends around us with project management skills who volunteered their time to help us organise the memorial service. Other friends kindly stepped in, offering to pay for the floral arrangements for both services.

This was the time when I wanted to shout to the world to stop. Just for one minute. I didn't want to have to choose what colour flowers, how many, and in which shape. What music was going to be played, who was going to speak, and who was performing. Reluctantly, armed with pen and paper, we slowly, painstakingly, wrote down the order of service for our daughter's memorial. I sat next to Karen and couldn't take my eyes off her. She held Charlotte's teddies, Heartsweet and Stitch, rocking backwards and forwards on her chair as if this would bring some kind of comfort.

We must have spent at least a couple of hours going over the order of service in minute detail. I felt completely drained and exhausted. By the end of it, our friends had everything they needed to know. They were such a godsend and great at taking control in a crisis. Karen and I had our list of things to do. There was a long pause once everyone had left as we sat together, alone in the kitchen, staring at one another in uncertainty. On the one hand, I felt relief at accomplishing the task of organising both services with my friends. On the other, I could not comprehend that it was our daughter's memorial we were arranging.

I wanted to reach out and heal the pain on my wife's face. I wanted to fix the problem, but there was an impenetrable wall of grief that prevented me from breaking through. I was so powerless. All I could do was stare at the floor, imagining a hole was about to open up and suck me in. I could not sleep at night. How could I rest when my daughter was dead?

I would lie in my bed, staring at the ceiling, recalling my last memories of Charlotte. How she would dance in front of the mirror in her bedroom, practicing incessantly. After picking her up from the *Billy Elliot* show, she used to snuggle under a blanket in the back of my car. She was tired but never too tired to smile as she sipped her hot chocolate. Sitting at the table after finishing dinner together, she would jump up and say, "Come on, Daddy, time to practise the show!"

I would pretend to know what I was doing as she ran through a dance scene from *Billy Elliot*. I would fumble my way through it and then we would both end up on the floor in a fit of giggles and laughter.

These happy memories kept her alive in my mind as I lay there, tears filling my eyes. How could this have happened to us? What a futile thought. I tried to be solution focused. I wanted to fight this pain and not let it defeat me. Charlotte's cremation was going to be on a Friday and the memorial on Sunday. This reminded me of a very popular old Gospel message, preached by the Rev. Tony Campolo around Easter time. It was a simple sermon – starting softly in volume and building in intensity, until you were completely involved, repeating the phrases in unison. 'It's Friday, but Sunday's coming'. The sermon went something like this:

It's Friday. Jesus is hanging on the cross, bloody and dying. But Sunday's coming.

It's Friday. The sky grows dark, the earth begins to tremble, and He who knew no sin became sin for us. Holy God who will not abide with sin pours out His wrath on that perfect sacrificial lamb who cries out, 'My God, My God. Why hast thou forsaken me?' What a horrible cry. But Sunday's coming.

It's Friday. And at the moment of Jesus' death, the veil of the Temple that separates sinful man from Holy God was torn from the top to the bottom because Sunday's coming.

It's Friday. Jesus is hanging on the cross, heaven is weeping and hell is partying. But that's because it's Friday and they don't know it, but Sunday's coming.

Now it's Sunday. And just about dawn on that first day of the week, there was a great earthquake. But that wasn't the only thing that was shaking because now it's Sunday. And the angel of the Lord is coming down out of heaven and rolling the stone away from the door of the tomb. Yes, it's Sunday, and the angel of the Lord is sitting on that stone. The guards posted at the tomb to keep the body from disappearing were shaking in their boots because it's Sunday. The lamb that was silent before the slaughter is now the resurrected lion from the tribe of Judah. For He is not here, the angel says. He is risen indeed.

It's Sunday and the crucified and resurrected Christ has defeated death, hell, sin and the grave. It's Sunday. And now everything has changed. It's the age of grace, God's grace poured out on all who would look to that crucified lamb of Calvary. Grace freely given to all who would believe that Jesus Christ died on the cross of Calvary, was buried and rose again, all because it's Sunday.

At the end of the message the pastor shouts out:

It's Friiidaaaay!

And you respond:

"But Sunday's coming!"

In my mind's eye I held onto this message that had inspired me for so long. My daughter's death was not in vain. This was not about redemption. This was about resurrection and she was born to dance with the angels. On that Friday I had to let her go so on the Sunday I could celebrate her life. She lived her life to the full and she was living her dream. Her life was cut short but what she achieved in such a short time not many of us would achieve in a lifetime. I lay awake at night thinking this through. My mind was still haunted by the image of Charlotte's face lying in the coffin. I felt evil whispering in my ear mocking my faith.

"How could a loving God allow this to happen to one of His followers?"

My thoughts were scrambling to hold onto the truth that bound my faith together. I frantically clung to my blood-stained cross. Even though the pain was too heavy to bear, I cried out to God for the strength to go on and the grace to carry my cross. It was Friday, but Sunday's coming…

The hearse pulled up outside the front of our house. We had cream coloured chrysanthemums form the words 'Gorgeous Charlotte' and a heart-shaped posy of cream and peach coloured roses. The heart was placed at the back of the hearse with 'Gorgeous' on one side of the coffin and 'Charlotte' on the other. Some of the neighbours lined up on the pavement to pay their respects as we followed in our cars behind the hearse. The journey to the crematorium was like a slow march.

My close friend Andy was driving my family in our car. I had known Andy for a long time and we were both best man at each other's weddings. Andy is a pastor and I asked him to give what was probably one of the hardest sermons he had to deliver in the twenty years he'd been a minister. He told me when he was preparing for the service he knew that words couldn't come near to expressing the pain or eradicating the wound. It was a great challenge for him but, at the same time, a great privilege. The loss of Charlotte had caused him to wrestle with God in prayer for answers and trust Him when he's silent. Our courage to cling to God despite the pain spurred him on.

As we arrived at the crematorium there were about fifty close friends and family waiting for us. I could not bear to look at anyone for fear of breaking down. A knot just kept tightening in my stomach. This felt like a sick joke being played out against us. Karen and I stood behind the hearse as the pallbearers lifted Charlotte's small maple wood coffin out and placed her on their shoulders. I had chosen six pallbearers, led by her two brothers, who looked like they alone were carrying the weight of the world on their shoulders.

Paul, who had been there for my family since the night of the accident, was one of the pallbearers. Paul had lost his dad when he was just eleven years old. He was too young to be a pallbearer at his father's funeral so I asked especially for him to be one at my daughter's. He began weeping as they slowly marched Charlotte into the crematorium and, by the time we were all sitting down, there wasn't a dry eye in the house.

I sat gazing at Charlotte's coffin, feeling completely detached, numb with pain. Could this really be happening? It was as though I was watching a tragic story in a movie, something that happened to other people, not to me or mine.

David, Karen's cousin, sang a song with his acoustic guitar that he had written in honour of Charlotte.

Dance like the Angels
Was it the way you danced or the sweetness of your smile?
That told us you were made for higher things?
Or was it something deeper, a light within your soul?
For you were born to dance before the King

And you shine like a star in the sky
As you dance like the angels tonight

Sometimes it seems too cruel, did you have to leave so soon?
So many things that we had planned to do
But what is that you're saying
As we struggle through these tears?
Are you calling us to come and dance with you?

And you shine like a star in the sky
As you dance like the angels tonight

For there's a calling, and a there's a higher stage
To live before the One who gave it all
And there's a greater dance that we were born to dance
For the King who is the Lover of our souls

And you shine like a star in the sky
As you dance like the angels tonight

This was a beautiful song and lyrics that reached out to me with hope. David had performed at our wedding and now it was so hard to believe he was singing to say goodbye to Charlotte. Andy preached a very personal, heartfelt sermon and managed to hold it together. A close friend of our family, Hazel, gave such a personal message expressing her love for Charlotte. She was shaking and so close to breaking down, but managed to describe Charlotte's fun-loving character in such an intimate way. Then Paul stood up and gave an honest and tearful message:

"People have been lost not knowing what to say. I do, it sucks and it's not fair…"

Paul just sobbed. He finished his tribute by saying:

"Charlotte, what can we say? You are twelve years old and are going to leave an incredible legacy. There are very few girls in this world who carried themselves as you did, always smiling, I look up to you…"

At that moment, with a press of a button her coffin was slowly lowered into the floor, as the U2 song '40' was being played, "I will sing, sing a new song, I will sing, sing a new song…"

I wanted to reach out and stop the coffin. I wanted to replay this whole god-awful drama and stop it from happening. But I couldn't. I was immobilized and there was nothing I could do. I was paralysed. All I could do was watch this nightmare unfold. God, if there was a new song, I couldn't hear it. I was deafened by my grief. God, where are you? How could you abandon me now? Have you forsaken me in my darkest hour?

# Chapter 4
## Beauty for Ashes

The memorial service celebrating the life of our gorgeous Charlotte began on Sunday, April 3, at the Dolphin School where Charlotte had spent many happy years of her school life, from reception class through to Year 6 (ages 4–11). She loved her time there. The school was housed inside the local Baptist church and the service was in the main church hall. As you walked in there was a large and radiant photo of Charlotte projected onto the wall behind the stage. In fact, there were photos of Charlotte blown up onto boards and positioned all over the church hall. The flowers from the cremation service were placed in the middle of the stage.

On one side there was a Hawthorn tree, given by the school in her memory, and on the other a large wooden cross. The service was led by the pastor, Nick Morris, and Jo Glen, the head teacher of Dolphin School. Jo had known Charlotte since she was a little girl.

I want to take you through this service as everyone who gave their tribute to Charlotte painted a bigger picture of who she was and what she meant to so many people. By three o'clock the church was full with about four hundred people. The congregation was made up of all the people who knew Charlotte and our family.

There were families we knew from the last fourteen years at Dolphin School. Some families came from the South London Dance Studios, where Charlotte attended since she was four years old. There were teachers and friends from The Charter Secondary School. Charlotte's new family from the *Billy Elliot* cast and crew attended. Last but not least, Karen's family and our friends. Noticeably, none of my side of the family was present. Pastor Nick stood up and welcomed everybody, ushering us to our feet to sing.

We all stood up slowly to sing one of Charlotte's favourite school assembly songs, the 'Travelling Song'. This was normally a jolly song to sing together. I tried to imagine Charlotte singing with her smiley face but all I could see was the way she looked lying in the coffin. Afterwards everyone sat down awkwardly and the atmosphere was tense.

Jo stood on the stage and led a tribute on behalf of the Dolphin School, Janet Clark (Deputy Head), and Charlotte's Year 6 class of 2010. She was so articulate as she spoke about Charlotte, and, although severely numbed by the shock, I did my best to engage with every word she said.

"Seated down there are Charlotte's Dolphin classmates – the class of 2010. Each has written a prayer – intermingled, interwoven and in their own words, form a collective Dolphin prayer with which we begin. Thank you for bringing Charlotte to this earth, one of my best friends, one of the kindest people, very talented in many ways. She will be known forever... she was beautiful and I loved her amazingly lovely smile and her ability never to say a bad word about anyone. Thank you for Charlotte always being cheerful and helping us all. Thank you that she always put others before herself... she was so kind to everyone and stood up for people. She was a very talented dancer and always kind, gentle and loving. Everyone loved her. Thank you for giving Charlotte the imagination she had...how she could see things differently. Thank you God for the time I saw Charlotte in *Billy Elliot* and we were able to talk afterwards. Thank you for the amazing things we did together – swinging on trees, rollerblading round the kitchen, going to sweetshops, having afternoon tea, giggling non-stop and sharing birthdays. Thank you for the memories of our crazy games – she'd always come up with the craziest, funniest ideas. Thank you for Wintershall and that we both loved being on stage together. Thank you for her huge imagination and creativity. She was a star. Thank you for wonderful times at Year 6 camp, sharing a tent; she lifted my spirits with our silly voices that no one else could do. I pray that her soul is blessed and with you, Father... I pray for her family... that they can carry on. Please bless the family as life goes on. Please help the Leatherbarrows in present times. I thank you that Charlotte is with you in the best place ever to be. I pray that the Leatherbarrows will always have hope and know that Charlotte is with you in heaven – with you forever. Charlotte, you were a dear friend and I will never forget you. I will never forget the joy in her smile. And so together, remembering Charlotte's joy, we join to say, 'Amen'."

Jo introduced Janet, the Deputy Head, who had known Charlotte since she was in reception class. She stepped up onto the stage and stood by Jo in front of the microphone. She spoke softly and soberly. I couldn't bear to look at the pained expression on Janet's face. I had to look away and my mind drifted. I only caught the last words of her speech.

"...As I spoke that day, I remember that Charlotte kept looking at me throughout – directly, openly, trustingly, and smilingly. In a way that I knew so well in an arresting, heart connected, beautiful way that you too will remember. Charlotte was passionate about people. She operated from a place of the greatest security and love. She was able to trust and reach out to others in an exceptional manner. Even as a toddler at the swimming pool, wearing her long beads and clutching her bag as she watched her brothers' swimming lessons. Her fascination with strangers was remarkable – looking at them intently, reading their faces and smiling at them with both her lips and her shining eyes. Later on her gifts of perception, understanding, and joy brought huge encouragement to us all at Dolphin, as well as to many people beyond these walls from all walks of life. Charlotte's sensitivity to people's feelings, needs and experiences was developed far beyond her years. She was quick to draw alongside the new person, the lonely, the sad, and the unsure. As well as joining in the games, the fun, the laughter and abundance. To be looked upon by Charlotte was to be fully and beautifully welcomed. Her face was a face of warm embrace, reflecting a heart of joy and love."

As Janet concluded her words, she stepped down from the stage. As the old wooden steps creaked under her feet there was complete silence in the room. Nobody moved. Jo gathered herself and continued her dedication to Charlotte. I lost concentration again. I looked around at the many familiar faces – some were smiling, some crying, others were just looking on with glazed eyes. This scene was all too surreal. Jo held up a crown of thorns made from the hawthorn tree, and a crown of flowers, as she stood in front of the wooden cross.

"And so enveloped by pain was he that from the cross he cried out, 'My God, my God, why have you forsaken me?' No answer was heard. It would be normal, natural and true if some of us and especially you, her close family, had joined your cry to that of the wounded God. In his place of desolation, He meets us today at the place of our deepest pain. Not with neat tidy answers but with his presence and with his love in the midst of which the crown of thorns remains very real. If Charlotte were a month, she would be for me the month of May, redolent of spring flowers and sunny days. Maypole dancing, a young girl in a cream dress, on her head a floral crown, with the maypole ribbons interweaving, as she dances as all our lives have interwoven with hers. Her life cut short where spring meets summer on the brink of her June. While we mourn the end of her last summer, her autumn, her winter, we rejoice today together at the memory of her perpetual spring. This was a girl so brimming with light and joy and sunshine that every essay she wrote (whatever the topic) would be so full of her favourite adjective – blissful. Miss Clark, Miss Baker and I would have to get very strict and stern and cross a few 'blissfuls' out. But blissful she was. And so we pray that the Holy Spirit, who came in the form of a dove, would, like the dove returning to the ark with the olive branch, alight on these thorns and start to fill the crown with colourful memories of Charlotte's perpetual spring. Flower by flower, memory by memory..."

Jo picked some of the flowers from the crown of flowers and placed them on the crown of thorns, "So that soon it looks like a crown of thorns, yes, underneath, a deep wound, but radiant with Charlotte's life, a spring crown. Charlotte danced as a flower fairy and the song of the May fairy is the song of the hawthorn tree. This hawthorn tree is a gift from Dolphin School to you, Karen and Neil."

Jo pointed to the tree standing at the side of the stage. I stared at it with such doubt, I could not relate to the white spring flower in bloom on this tree. I felt like I had entered a permanent winter and I would never be warm again.

"Yes, there are earthly crowns that Charlotte, for all her many gifts, will not now wear and we lament those today. But they were crowns that the Bible tells us 'will not last'. But after the pain and desolation of the cross, represented by this crown (thorns), comes the glorious, eternal light of resurrection represented by this crown (flowers). And today, resurrected, Charlotte wears 'the crown of life that God has promised to those who love him'. And she did, Charlotte really loved Him. Jesus was her Shepherd and her Guide. 'And when the Chief Shepherd appears', it says in the first book of Peter, 'you will receive the crown of glory that will never fade away.' This is a Celtic blessing that Miss Baker (the other Deputy Head) gave me. 'Life given is a gift from God and life withheld is the gateway to eternity'. Lord, we thank you for the gift of Charlotte's life and we thank you that you, the Chief Shepherd, now carry her like a precious lamb through the gateway to eternity. In Jesus' name, Amen."

Jo looked down, smiled, and then graciously walked off the stage. We all stood up and sang another of Charlotte's favourite Dolphin School songs called, 'Lord of the Sea and Sky'. I mimed the words as nothing came out, my mouth was dry. Such beautiful words spoken about my daughter but I couldn't feel anything. Next, a lovely lady called Marian walked up to the microphone to give a tribute on behalf of the *Billy Elliot* show.

"Charlotte was the perfect example of what makes the children at *Billy Elliot* so special. She was energetic, enthusiastic, passionate and completely dedicated to her performance in the show. Above all, she was a very talented young dancer and actress. Charlotte had a real spark for life and although impeccably behaved at the theatre, she was definitely spirited. With just a little touch of cheekiness to bring out her character! She was a true joy to have around. Although I'm sure Karen, Neil and her brothers can probably tell us tales of when she didn't behave so angelically, she was always mature and focused about her performance. I remember Charlotte being cast in the show as we all thought she had the most fabulous name for the stage. During rehearsals for the show there were two Charlottes joining us. So, she became affectionately known as 'Charlie Wheelbarrow' by Alan, our Children's Dance Captain. But he assures me this was not a judgement on her dance ability! In fact, I've heard from the other girls that Charlotte would regularly entertain them during rehearsals by performing a supermodel catwalk up on Pointe, which is by no means easy! Charlotte was so excited at her first tutu fitting, and our costume assistant, Hannah, clearly remembers how infectious her positivity was. However, one piece of costume became Charlotte's nemesis. There was certainly no love lost between Charlotte and the T   -shirt she wore prior to the quick costume change the girls have in the musical number 'Shine'. Despite being brilliant at the change, Charlotte was convinced that the T-shirt had a mind of its own and purposely got tangled around her head every night! In the end, Sharon, our wardrobe mistress, took pity on her and found Charlotte a new, better-behaved top. Charlotte also had a little routine that she would perform in the wing with Wendy, our deputy wardrobe mistress. During a costume change Wendy would hold out Charlotte's bobble hat for her to put on. But it would have been too simple just to take it. So Charlotte would always bend down so that she could 'duck' into the hat without using her hands. This became their ritual every performance! The Ballet Girl chaperones, Kim and Cherida, have told me what a great example Charlotte was to the other girls in how she behaved. It is a testament to Karen and Neil that she was such a polite and courteous girl. Everyone I've spoken to has mentioned Charlotte's beaming smile that was so infectious to all around her and that will be one of our lasting memories of her. Charlotte was fabulous in the role of Sharon Percy, being one of the smallest girls to ever take it on. We were so thrilled that she had accepted another contract to stay with the show for another term. I know that she would have been equally as brilliant in her new role, and I know Charlotte was looking forward to the new challenge. Charlotte was a true star in the making and I've no doubt that she had a bright future ahead of her. But she also had already achieved so much by performing in a West End show at such a young age. I know the cast and technical team at *Billy* will miss Charlotte dreadfully, particularly the Ballet Girls and her team. But for *Billy Elliot*, she will always shine in our memories."

A tearful Marian stepped down from the stage, another uplifting speech, another painful reminder of my loss. Now I was starting to feel agitated sitting still. I wanted to stand up and scream, "God, why Charlotte?"

Zoe and Emma, Charlotte's dance teachers, stood and walked up to the front to make a speech on behalf of everyone at the South London Dance Studios. Rachel, one of Charlotte's faithful friends, was with them. I found it hard to focus when I just wanted to get up and walk away. I only managed to catch the tail end of Zoe's speech.

"...And Neil of course was official chauffeur to the little *Billy Elliot* star, driving her back from long days and evenings at the theatre in Victoria, with their journey home starting off with stories ten to the dozen before exhaustion gradually set in. Karen and Neil shared in Charlotte's great joy as she succeeded in what she loved to do and they supported her every step of the way. Also cheering on Charlotte were, of course, her brothers, her Nan-Ann and her close friends. Charlotte's friends at SLDS were so proud of her achievements. She led the way in dance festivals and auditions, reporting back to her friends on her experiences and achievements. She was a great team member, being able to work well with others and blend in or stand out in a group dance as appropriate. Charlotte was a gel amongst the girls at SLDS and her friends' touching tributes over the last two weeks are testimony to Charlotte's place in their hearts where she will remain forever."

Zoe managed to compose herself and allowed Rachel to nervously recite her poem for Charlotte.

"A special quality that shined, my beautiful friend Charlotte. We laughed together, we played together and dressed up. We danced together and shared many wonderful times together. My memories of you, Charlotte, are treasures. It makes me sad we've been parted. But now you are with our heavenly Father, in His loving arms. I love you, my special friend, and nothing can take that away."

Rachel moved aside to let Emma speak.

"My first memory of Charlotte was the night I started teaching for Grafton at St. Saviour's church hall. I remember seeing her and thinking she was the spitting image of me when I was her age. Not in the face, but she had the same little muscled legs and curly hair. This became our thing, she was miniature me and I remember telling her countless times she would grow. In time she would learn to like her muscular legs because they look quite good with heels".

Everyone laughed softly and Emma continued, her voice trembling.

"For me the thing I'm going to miss most is the little things she did that always made me smile. Some of the exercises we did, I couldn't even look at her because I knew if I did, she'd have that look on her face. That cheeky mischievous look and we'd both burst out laughing and that's something I'll always remember every time I think of Charlotte. I remember when Charlotte got into *Billy Elliot*. I was so proud of her but at the same time I thought about how much I was going to miss having her around. But I didn't have to miss her because she would send me little cards to the dance school telling me how much she was having fun and how much she missed my classes. Even though I always said thank you, she will never truly know how much that meant to me. She truly was a kind and caring person, thoughtful towards her teachers and towards her friends. She loved to share her knowledge and experiences. Charlotte had some very close friends at SLDS and here are their thoughts. We all think of Charlotte as our sister, she was our good friend to dance with, have fun with, and confide in. We all have so many special memories of Charlotte and we will never forget them. Charlotte was so talented and clever, and she had a beautiful smile that would light up a room the moment she walked in. She was bubbly and cheeky and we all loved being with her. Charlotte, we love you and we'll miss you so much. I really hope that one day I'll get to see Charlotte again and she can show me that funny Charleston move she always loved to do. So for now it's not goodbye, but as Charlotte would often say, or write to me in her cards, see ya!"

Hesitantly, she stepped back to allow Zoe to give a final word.

"On a personal note, I will truly miss Charlotte's energy and enthusiasm. I have met very few people or students who so consistently invest one hundred percent effort into everything they do and have such a consistently positive attitude. This really did make Charlotte a pleasure to see at the dance studios four or five times a week as well as to teach. I will miss Charlotte's great zest for life and, of course, I will miss watching her talent grow as it undoubtedly would have done. Since first meeting Charlotte when she was four, we've been through a lot together. She was one of my very first students who wanted to take dance more seriously than as a hobby. And I couldn't have wished for a more lovely and appreciative student to find my way with. The only one thing Charlotte could not do for me was grow – just a little bit was all I would ask her for. This was our ongoing joke but in reality I wouldn't have changed her for the world. She was the perfect little dancing package with a very special talent and a very bright future. We'll never know why Charlotte was taken from us. But what we do know is that wherever she is and whoever she is with, she will be lighting up that place with her joy and laughter. She will undoubtedly be showing off all her dances, entertaining with her stories, and telling her new friends about her guinea pigs. They are so lucky to have her and we only wish we'd had her with us for longer. Goodbye, Charlotte, we will miss you so much." Zoe's voice faded away as they returned to their seats.

Next was a young man whom I had known for a long time and who had written a great love song that our family loved. Daniel Bedingfield stood up on stage alongside his acoustic guitarist, Eric, who was sitting on a chair. Briefly, he introduced himself and his relationship to my family. Then he stood back and took a deep breath to sing his song 'I'm Never Gonna Leave Your Side.' There was a hush over the congregation as Daniel sang it with such depth of feeling and, as always, pitch-perfect. A beautiful song and sung so passionately.

Then it was my brother-in-law's turn to stand up behind the microphone. Mark, Karen's older brother, stood tall, a big guy, but softly spoken. "There's a nice easy act to follow." The congregation laughed appreciatively.

"I envisaged Charlotte being gracious enough to say something at my send-off but I never, ever thought it would be this way round..."

My mind trailed off again. I was anticipating the worst. I knew we were going to play a tribute film of Charlotte's life and I didn't know if I could stay seated without breaking down in front of everyone. My feelings were about to overflow like a flood bursting the banks of a river. I fought to hold myself together.

"Finally," Mark concluded, "I would like to pay tribute to the Leatherbarrow family, to say how incredibly proud I am to be a part of this family. My super-cool sister. Neil, you're a legend; Luke, hyper-intelligent; and Jason, supernatural. Of course, Charlotte is going to live on in our hearts forever. If we can each have a fraction of the positive impact on others as she did then this world will be a better place. We are going to see Charlotte's life in pictures now – so get your tissues out."

Projected onto the wall behind the stage, a ten minute film danced before our eyes, an outpouring of Charlotte's life in photograph and video footage. There is always the breaking point. People were no longer able to contain their grief as slowly the sounds of sobbing and whimpering built to a crescendo throughout the hall. The dam had broken and all the heartache was spilling forth. Our dear friends from Khaki Films, Casey and Zoe, had spent many hours piecing together this very moving tribute to Charlotte. They had known her since she was nine years old, when she had first auditioned for a role in their movie, *Dance Like the Flower Fairies*. Casey and Zoe stood at the back of the church filming the service, giving us a lasting record of our grief.

Next to grace the stage was our beautiful South African friend, Mpho, as she sang Natasha Bedingfield's song 'Wild Horses', accompanied by Luke Smith on keyboards. Mpho managed to hold back the tears and sing so smoothly, her voice so gentle and easy on the ear. The lyrics of the song were very appropriate, describing the freedom you desire, just as Charlotte expressed it when she danced before you. Last but not least, our family tribute to Charlotte. First up was Luke, smartly dressed with courage pinned to his jacket like a well-deserved medal.

"Hi, everyone. In case you didn't know, I'm Charlie's little big bro. This is just a poem that I wrote and it really sums up my feelings about Charlotte and our situation. Hopefully I won't cry any more or I'm going to ruin this new jacket..."

Luke paused and cleared his throat.

"Heaven's new angel arrived the other day.

I thought she just popped in but now she's there to stay.

A star to everyone and anyone who saw her,

Felt warm inside like a sauna.

A sister to me, physically she's gone. Spiritually, she'll be in my heart forever long. Until the day we meet,

I'll treasure the laughs, your wonderful thoughts as treats.

You're the sweetest thing in our lives.

I'm just glad I have twelve beautiful years to remember you by.

Some say rest in peace, but you're not able. You'll dance in heaven, Heaven's new angel."

Luke was greeted with a spontaneous applause as he sat down next to his brother, Jason, who sat there quietly staring at the floor. The congregation were still weeping, wiping their tears away with tissues, immersed in every word that was spoken. Karen and I stepped up to the microphone together. Karen, so brave and composed as she took first turn to speak. I took a long look around at the people representing our life in London for the last fourteen years. I wasn't really listening to what Karen was saying. I couldn't, otherwise I wouldn't have been able to speak myself, until the moment Karen turned to look at me and said, "She even knew the type of man she wanted to marry. She wanted somebody very fit, dark hair and green eyes…"

Everyone laughed in unison and now I focused my attention on her.

"She knew the right time when she decided she would have children. When she could bring them up and still have a career. She knew the financial sacrifice we made as a family to keep her dancing. It was a sacrifice and we often went without a holiday or something so she could experience her time with the National Youth Ballet and all the things she had to do. She knew that and she appreciated it. Someone described her in one of our cards as being rather like an enchanted pixie. Or a real life fairy from a favourite bedtime story, or the merry month of May that everyone looks forward to. She was my tulip fairy. Charlotte would leave notes and poems around the house for me always. Saying things like she'd missed me during a day at school or she liked her lunch. Or, if she was out, how much she would like Neil and I to have a romantic evening together. When she was in her bed, she couldn't bear to be alone so she would text me while I was downstairs. I have had an extraordinary journey with this twelve-year-old girl and it has come to a brutal end. She will not be a teenager; she will not be the young, beautiful successful woman, wife and mother. We feel very robbed. Her twelve years were lived to the full. She fulfilled a dream that some of us in this room will not fulfil in a lifetime. I leave you with these words at her final audition at *Billy Elliot*. She came out and she said, 'Well, Mama, that's it. I gave one hundred per cent. I gave everything I had all of the time. I held nothing back, I threw myself into it. So if they don't want me, if I don't get cast, then it's okay because it meant that it wasn't for me as I have nothing more to give'. She did get the part, we know the story. She was a great example – she wasn't perfect, she was messy. But she was our daughter and our lives will not be the same without her. We are left with the most physical ache and pain in our hearts."

Karen stepped back and it was my turn next. I inhaled and blew out a deep breath to begin the hardest speech a father could give.

"I guess I'll finish then. Well, first of all, Karen and I and the family – well, words aren't really enough... The support, the overwhelming support we've had from you guys has just been immense. From all the cards we've received, all the Facebook messages, text messages, emails, phone calls, flowers, it's been overwhelming. We really want to thank you for being there for us during this time. Even to make today happen and everybody who has been involved with that, as you can see a lot of time, energy and effort have gone

65

into making this day happen. We are so grateful. You are beautiful people. Thank you.

"I know there are many fathers here today and fathers with daughters. I believe when our children are in trouble, it's the fathers who come to the rescue. Like last summer, we were having a typical holiday in Cornwall; it was freezing cold and pouring with rain. But Charlotte and I still decided to go in the sea. It was a bit rough that day and the riptide was pulling us out. And then the waves kept coming over Charlotte's head and they were dragging her under. So I grabbed her and kept her head above water and made it back to the shore safely. When our daughters are in trouble, it's the fathers who come to the rescue. We don't need a superhero's costume to know who the real heroes are, right? Fathers, we know who we are. Mothers, you may not realise it, but we do. Except when your daughter is killed in a road accident and you can't rescue her any more. You're left feeling powerless and completely helpless. You just can't get your head around it. You can't find any meaning from such a meaningless accident.

"But Charlotte would not want you to remember her life as a tragedy. She didn't want your pity in life and she wouldn't want it in her death, either. She lived her life to the full. She worked hard to achieve her goals and realise her dreams. She reached out, she gave back, and she made a difference, setting an example for others to follow. This is why we are forming the Charlotte Leatherbarrow Foundation, to enable other young dancers, actors, and singers to perform to the best of their ability and with distinction in their character. What you see in a performance on stage may only take minutes to accomplish. But what you don't see are the countless hours of time, energy and money that go into making that performance look so good. We want to give our talented young people the opportunity to dance when nobody is watching and the freedom to dance like nobody is watching.

"In light of the austerity cuts we are experiencing right now, the performing arts, sadly, are all too often seen as a luxury and just for our entertainment. When my daughter danced, she danced with such grace and confidence. She commanded your respect when she performed. I never had this kind of confidence when I was a young boy. We need young performers in shows like *Billy Elliot* to carry on because they don't just bring entertainment; they bring a message of hope and transformation for a new generation. Charlotte made a difference in life and we want to continue making that difference in her memory. Charlotte was our *Billy Elliot* story. We managed her on a shoestring of a budget and enabled her dream of dancing on the West End stage. So we invite you to help us build this foundation. Help us build a legacy that Charlotte would be proud of. I will never forget my gorgeous daughter and I'm gonna make sure you don't either. Thank you for coming."

As I finished, everybody rose to their feet and started to applaud. We ushered Luke and Jason onto the stage with us and took the time to look around at the congregation. On the Friday we cremated Charlotte and watched her body disappear but on the Sunday we remembered her soul. We cherished our memories of her, we laughed, we cried, and now we rose together like a family. We stood strong and held each other. I felt an overpowering sense of peace and unity with these people.

Rising from Charlotte's ashes there was a real aroma of beauty in this place. Out of her story there emerged a beautiful life. Even out of the darkness in which my grief held me, I could still find the light of hope for my daughter's resurrection. I cannot give up now, I thought. I love my daughter too much for that to happen. My belief in a God of love had become a part of me for so long and my family had lived and thrived from knowing that to love is to give. I could not turn my back on Him now. God was a part of me as much as I was a part of Him. There was nowhere I could go where He hadn't already been.

# Chapter 5
## Nowhere to Run

The county of Somerset – a beautiful landscape of rolling hills and deep valleys where they brewed scrumpy cider and the locals spoke with a thick country accent. This was to be my new home and I was full of hope, desiring to make a clean start. I still had a couple of weeks left of summer holidays to settle into my new home, Penrhyn flats at the top of North Hill, overlooking the pleasant beach and town centre. Minehead was in every way a breath of fresh air. My dad was busy covering the Miss West Somerset contest being held down at the Lido on Minehead seafront. He also helped us secure a summertime job with one of the organisers who owned the local Wellington Hotel.

My brother and I stacked empty, smelly beer bottles into dirty old crates. The job didn't pay very much but it did give a small measure of self-esteem to think I was going some way to pay my way to help my dad. But if the days were a relief, the nights were still tormenting, full of recurring nightmares where I was chased by a dark, menacing figure. He would imprison me with a heavy weight, crushing my chest, before throwing me down a bottomless black hole. I would fight my way back to consciousness, struggling to catch my breath and soaked in sweat. My dad would try to comfort me, but feeling helpless, he sought assistance.

The local doctor immediately prescribed a liquid form of valium to help me sleep. No matter where I ran, the psychological damage of the past always seemed to catch up with me and haunt me in my sleep. Now here I was becoming addicted to a drug I'd already seen destroy my mother's mental health. In a matter of months, even though I was prescribed a nightly dose of ten millilitres of valium, I progressed to drinking it from the bottle and still the drug couldn't keep my nightmares at bay. To top it all, this wasn't the only drug that had become habitual in strong doses.

In my alter ego as a petty thief, before I would 'go out on a job', I used to open up a large tin of industrial glue, take a tea towel and put it over my head. For about five minutes I would inhale the sweet smelling glue, which sent me into overdrive and gave me an energy and confidence to do things I wouldn't normally do. I would scramble up drainpipes at the back of an empty house, crawl through a small window, and then run down to open up the front door. I let my accomplices in to steal and inflict damage on the homes of unsuspecting people that my gang had been targeting for weeks.

In my first year of living in Minehead, I didn't rekindle my deviant lifestyle. I was trying to turn over a new leaf. I was twelve years old and had discovered something far more interesting. Girls! *Grease* was the big movie of the year and I escorted my first girlfriend, Kate, to see it at the Regal Cinema. We sat at the back where nobody could see us, and halfway through the movie, I managed to put my arm around her. I kept looking to see if she wanted to kiss, but she seemed more interested in watching the movie through to the end.

Finally, I took the plunge and leaned over to kiss Kate on the lips. We were both very nervous and she bit my lip so hard that it started to bleed. We left the cinema red-faced with embarrassment. The next day at school Kate promptly finished the short-lived romance between us. I wasn't the only one chasing after romance. My dad had a girlfriend or two until he met Anne. She was ten years younger than him, an attractive woman with a strong, determined-looking face, hazel-brown eyes, and she perfected the 'sixties look' with a brown beehive-like hairstyle and make-up to match.

After visiting on weekends for a few months, Anne moved in with us. A move that proved very difficult for Lance to adjust to. He had already made room for me and now, with Anne, he didn't feel as close to our dad any more. I liked Anne enough to share our fondness for the music of *Grease*. She also introduced me to The Bee Gees' 'Saturday Night Fever' and disco dancing. For once in my life, I wasn't in the middle of a conflict. Instead, I found myself caught in between my brother and stepmother's verbal skirmishes.

My personal view on marriage was that first marriages looked hard enough to make work but second marriages were even harder. My mother's second marriage, to Michael, had ended with her taking refuge in a battered wives home and now I hoped my dad's relationship with Anne would be better than my mum's experience. Lance resented Anne for taking his father's attention away from him. For me, the world had just started to look like a better place to live in when my dad dropped a bombshell on us both. He sat Lance and me down for a serious talk and made it very clear that he was going to marry Anne the following spring in 1980.

That wasn't so shocking but he also stated explicitly that Anne would always come first in his life and we would be relegated to second place. This unequivocal point resonated throughout my whole body and the statue of a father figure that I held on a pedestal suddenly came crashing down around me. Now I felt even less than a second-class citizen and destined to become the victim of another's selfish behaviour.

Meanwhile, in my alter ego, I had joined up with a gang led by some older teenagers. During the winter of 1979 we were making a general nuisance of ourselves by ringing people's doorbells and then make a run for it. We used to call this game 'knockdown ginger'. This progressed to stealing empty bottles from doorsteps, claiming the refund on them, or using the bottles to smash the promenade's streetlights at night. The news of my father's impending marriage to Anne just seemed to refuel the resentment and anger within me. I hit the self-destruct button, ready to cause carnage and chaos to myself and to all those around me. Bizarrely, I'd already hit the front page of the local newspaper in February 1980, for being part of the only teenage team to win the local pancake race, held in the town centre. At the same time, Anne was causing a stir by becoming the manager of Bealesons, the new department store in town.

In March, my dad and Anne sealed their commitment with their marriage. I don't remember much about that day because I had sneaked off with a bottle of champagne and quietly drunk myself into a stupor. At the end of the day, I passed out and was found on a couch in the reception area. But something much more sinister was about to make the headline news. My gang had stepped up its anarchic attack on society by breaking into cars and houses. We stole whatever we found of value and hoarded it in the den we had made in a derelict old house.

One night, we broke into a car that happened to belong to the owner of the Minehead Football Club. I was playing lookout while the older members stole a video camera and thousands of scratch cards that had a top prize of £50,000 for the lucky winner. We each took a thousand cards and went home hoping to find the prize-winning card. I spent the whole night sitting up in bed, feverishly scratching through one thousand cards only to find I had won £12. I met up with the rest of the gang the next day to discover they hadn't won any money at all.

None of them wanted to claim the prize money for fear that they would be recognised by someone at the club. So I decided to go in and claim the £12. That proved to be the worst mistake of my criminal career. Someone at the club recognised me with the stolen cards and reported it to the police. I stayed out late that night celebrating the miserly winnings with my gang, drinking shandy. When I finally made it home, I'll never forget that feeling I had as I turned the last corner. As I passed the war memorial on North Hill leading onto St. Michael's Road, there, parked in front of Penrhyn flats, was a police car.

I stopped dead in my tracks, panicking about what might happen. I played out several potential scenarios in my mind.

I even contemplated running away and never coming back. I decided to try and bluff it. I would pretend that a stranger sold me some of the scratch cards on the street and make up a description of a fictional character. I had done this once before back in Hullbridge after my gang had broken into a supermarket and set the alarm off. The boys dared me to make up a story to the police when they arrived at the scene of the crime. They knew I was reckless enough to rise to the challenge.

I quickly hid behind the building stripped off the fly suit I was wearing, revealing a different set of clothes so nobody would recognise me. Then I waited outside the front of the supermarket. When the police car came tearing down the road I flagged them down and told them I saw two tall guys in hoodies running off. I pointed to the direction they had fled. The police, swayed by my fake story, sped off chasing two hooded guys that didn't even exist. Keeping this in mind, with a smug look on my face and a swagger in my step, I strolled into my flat to face the music. My thoughts of pulling off the biggest performance of my life soon faded.

There were two police officers waiting for me in the lounge. My dad and Anne both gave me stern looks and told me to sit down. All the confidence that I'd mustered outside seemed to drain away along with my fake story. The more I tried to convince the officers of what happened, the more foolish I looked. It was as though they already knew the truth and were just waiting for me to confess. My time was up. I had spun my last web of deceit. I just wanted the ground to swallow me up. It was time to take off the mask and reveal my alter ego. My plan had all gone so horribly wrong. This wasn't how it was supposed to end. I wanted to bring shame on my stepfather, not embarrassment for my dad or my new stepmother.

I could only imagine the ridicule my dad had to take from colleagues at work when he had to report my story for the *West Somerset Free Press*. This incident had only begun to unravel the details of my criminal life. The two older members of the gang were taken into custody and later they were to be prosecuted for fourteen different criminal offences. I was only thirteen years old and, together with two others, we had to wait to hear the outcome of our demise. There was much speculation between us on what could happen. We had heard many gruelling stories about 'Borstal', the young offender's prison that delinquents like us were sent to[1].

In the end, the Crown Prosecution Service decided not to prosecute, deeming we were too young to be sent down. We were given a caution instead. This news changed my world as I was so scared of where I might have ended up. My life, had I gone to prison, would have turned out so differently. I can still remember the day when I stood in front of every authority figure in my life at that time. My father, my school headmaster, and the chief of police warned me of the consequences if I ever broke the law again. I would have been sent straight to prison. I realised what a reprieve this was and that my sentence was not to be carried out behind bars. But

[1] Many years later I watched a movie called *Scum*, which was based on real life inside this very prison, and confirmed the stories I had been told.

I also learned how bad news travelled fast, especially within a small community like Minehead.

My sentence was to be served in the community where everybody knew who I was and what I had done. I felt like the lowest of the low. The teachers at school looked down on me; I was banned from the local football club and people in the local shops I frequented held me in contempt. Most of all my family was disgusted with me. The message was clear – I was an outcast. My dad tried to reform my rebellious ways by forcing me to go to church on Sundays, but there I felt the same contempt from the churchgoers. If Jesus wanted me for a sunbeam, he needed to send somebody else.

Whatever message they had to bring, it flew right over my head. Instead, I spent my time disrupting the service. One time, I sat behind an elderly member of the church, wearing her Sunday best and a very nice hat, too. When the preacher was about to reach the climax of his sermon, with precise timing, I pulled a pin out of her hat and swiftly poked her up the bottom. She immediately screamed out loud and spoiled the preacher's final revelation. Everybody turned their heads and stared at me as if they had been repulsed by an odious smell. The scene ended with me being chastised and led out to the back of the church by the scruff of the neck.

At school I had worked my way up to the top stream but now my callous behaviour invited my teacher's scorn and derision. My work began to suffer for it. The only subject I seemed to be able to focus my boundless energy on was drama. I had previously saved the drama teacher's daughter from choking to death. She was having an epileptic fit in the school playground. I grabbed a plastic spoon and put it in her mouth to stop her from choking on her own tongue. This appeared to put me in my teacher's good books. So she picked me for a special project that only a handful of students were chosen to do.

During the summer of 1980, the BBC was in town filming a children's drama called *The Bells of Astercote*. It was going to be a one-off adaptation of Penelope Lively's ghost story about two children who move to a village that was abandoned during the Black Death. They were filming it on location in Porlock, a small village just over the other side of North Hill. A group of students from Minehead Middle School had been chosen to perform background parts in the drama. This meant we had two days off school and were able to hang out with the cast. The boy and girl playing the main roles were very well-spoken and boasted about the films they had been working on.

They did catch my attention for a short time with descriptions of starring roles as little Jawas in *Star Wars*. I envied their privileged lifestyles and dreamed of becoming a movie star myself. But what propelled my self-esteem into the stratosphere was acting in a scene where I sat right in front of the camera and had to react to some bad news given during a town hall meeting. At the end of shooting the scene I overheard the director tell the producer, "That kid is a real natural," pointing right at me.

Those few words of encouragement were such a huge boost to my confidence. Despite the infamy I had earned in the local community, I was riding high on cloud nine for weeks. On December 23, 1980, *The Bells of Astercote* was shown on BBC1. My brother and I were visiting our mum for

Christmas. This was a proud moment for me to watch my newfound love of acting on screen and show off to my mum.

In October that same year, my mum had tied the knot with her third husband, Gerry, a car mechanic. He was a tall, burly guy with a bushy beard and dark glasses. She had also renewed her love for the supernatural with Gerry and both attended regular séances at a local spiritualist church.

I was always involved with sports at school, a defender in football, a scrum-half in rugby and quite good at athletics as well. I was fast, a sprinter. On my very first sports day, the annual athletics contest at school, I was six years old and the night before I had a nasty bout of diarrhoea. I still didn't feel great the next morning but was determined to run in the sprint race. I was doing my best to hold it together when my race started. But let's say I was very eager to finish it, so eager that I did a 'Forrest Gump'. I didn't stop at the finish line even though I had won. I just kept running straight for the school toilets.

That's when I first discovered I was good at sprinting and usually won the one hundred metres race every year, until that is, the West Somerset Comprehensive School. Every young person aged thirteen and upwards from the neighbouring villages and towns attended this school. Sports day became far more competitive and I met my nemesis in the one hundred metres. Chris Simpkins. He was very fast, a strong and athletic figure, and he beat me every time we raced against each other. He was so admired for his athletic prowess; he won a place in the British Junior Athletics Team. I soon lost my place in the football and rugby team too as the competition became so fierce.

This loss of approval just seemed to bond the bitter roots that were growing up inside me, strangling any hope or desire of championing my ambitions in life. My acting skills were quenched as I failed to make it into the new school play. Life in Penrhyn flats was turning sour too. Anne did not have any children of her own so it was understandable that she didn't really want to take on two teenagers. Lance was avoiding any confrontation with Anne so they just seemed to tolerate each other's presence in the home. I was still grounded and under a curfew. I spent most evenings in my bedroom, just to steer clear of the sharp comments from my stepmother. She couldn't bear living in the same place as a juvenile delinquent.

This acidic concoction would soon boil over and my verbal retaliation was counteracted with feline opposition from Anne. I discovered that having a physical fight with a grown man was a lot simpler than having one with a grown woman. Anne seemed to exploit the fact that I wouldn't dare hit a woman after what my mum had experienced with Michael. She would start off with a verbal confrontation then launch into a neurotic rage and literally try to scratch my eyes out. I kept her at bay by forcibly holding her back. After the conflict ended, her arms were bruised from where I held her.

When my dad returned home from work, Anne would tell him an exaggerated story. Before I could even explain my side, my father instantly smacked me across the face. The force of his blow knocked me to the floor. He warned me that if I ever laid a finger on her again, I would find myself worse off. He reiterated his love for Anne was greater than that for his own son. Frustrated with the outcome, I realised how much more crafty women were in the way they did combat. This was a battle I couldn't win as the odds were stacked against me. And now that my father had resorted to physical violence, I had lost all respect for his parental authority.

The breakdown in the relationship with my dad and Anne just seemed to exacerbate my violent nightmares and fear of the dark. The incessant nightmare of being forced under pressure and not able to escape would be the moment when I woke up. Except I could not wake up from this one, I was living it. I felt like my back was against the wall and I had nowhere to run. In desperation I turned to my mum, confiding in her on the phone. This provided me with a way of escape.

In the summer of 1981, my Mum and Gerry visited Lance and me in Minehead. During this time, Gerry tried to convince us that spiritualism was good and not evil. He explained that his guide spirit would only speak positive messages through him. I didn't understand and asked him for a demonstration. So we sat and waited for his guide spirit to come and manifest itself. Gerry bowed his head in meditation. Suddenly, I began to feel a pressure on the back of my head trying to push me down into unconsciousness. Just when I felt like I was going under, Gerry poked his head up and said, "It was no good, my guide spirit was not going to speak."

I was petrified, feeling like my recurring nightmares had just become a reality. I looked at my mum in disbelief and thought, 'what kind of a nutter have you married now?' By the time I returned to school in September the conflicts at home were intensifying. My mum wanted me to come and live with her and Gerry. I felt trapped and my mum was offering me the only way out. I had a choice to stay or leave but my emotions were overwhelming me. I felt I had to get away whenever conflict reared its ugly head.

A domestic battle had been raging all around me for too long. All I wanted was some peace, some respite from the war on the home front. I didn't really know what I was going to parachute into, but the territory looked a lot friendlier than the one I was living in. Here I was again plotting my escape, except this time with my mum. Together we arranged for her to pick me up from school after my dad dropped me off before going to work. Then we would go back to the Penrhyn flat to pack my stuff and leave for my new home in Maylandsea, Essex.

Everything went to plan. I left Minehead without my dad or Anne knowing. I wasn't broken-hearted this time. What I did feel was numb and desensitized. My life seemed to be fleeing from one conflict to another, a shadow relentlessly in pursuit of my soul. I had just turned fifteen and felt the strength of my will to go on fighting was failing. I was running on empty. Driving in my new stepfather's car, I closed my eyes. In my mind's eye, I was driving into a long dark tunnel with no light at the end. I guess this is what psychologists would call depression. I didn't care what it was so long as it wasn't another fight.

# Chapter 6
## All That You Can Leave Behind

The flowers were beginning to wither and die, the smell was beginning to fade. Everywhere, there were so many tributes written for Charlotte and the family as I looked around my house. The biggest and the brightest were a huge bouquet of cream roses with a card signed by Sir Elton John, David and Zachery, with love and sympathy. Sir Elton had written the music for *Billy Elliot* and had heard about our family tragedy. The flowers sat in front of our fireplace in the lounge next to fifty red roses bought by our good friend Daniel, who didn't want to be overshadowed by Sir Elton.

One of the most touching sentiments were a bunch of tulips sent from our friends in Amsterdam, with a card saying, 'Your Amsterdam Youth Group'. These were young people we had known for over twenty years and were so kind and thoughtful to remember us. It was so hard to believe all these messages were for Charlotte instead of me or Karen. This was so unnatural. The shock somehow acting as a natural anaesthetic trying to numb the pain – but the intensity of emotion would break through, sweeping over me. This was so wrong and yet so real and there was nothing I could do to change this. I couldn't change the outcome by shouting, "Stop! Let's go back and start again!"

This reminded me of one of the most intense scenes I've seen in a war movie. In *Saving Private Ryan* there is a hand-to-hand fight between an American and a German soldier. The American pulls out a knife but the German is physically bigger and stronger than him. He turns his own knife on him and forcefully, slowly, pushes the knife into his heart. As if to bring some kind of comfort, the German tells him to 'hush' as he kills him. The American panics and shouts at him to stop, but it is too late.

Like the American soldier, I felt helpless. There was nothing I could do to stop my pain or my family's, there was no prevention. Karen and I spent hours sitting in Charlotte's bedroom as though time had stood still. All her things were in the same place. We touched nothing. Charlotte kept a wipe-clean board on the wall by her bed where she had written 'notes to self' of how she had performed in the *Billy Elliot* show and school notes for homework. Things like this became such precious keepsakes that we kept them exactly the same as they were when she was alive.

This was such a role reversal, a twisted reality. I was treasuring all the things that reminded me of Charlotte in her death instead of her keeping things to remind her of me in mine. Every possession I owned, every familiar place I visited conjured up such happy memories, only to be brutally torn apart by the reminder of my loss. There was a rich store of Charlotte's twelve years on this earth spent living in the same area and going to the same school for seven of those years.

These memories came when we went to the old fashioned sweet shop to buy Charlotte some treats because she had a real sweet tooth; frequent visits to the Blue Mountain Café for my favourite cup of coffee while Charlotte would enjoy a cup of hot chocolate; going to the park where she learnt to ride a bike, climb trees, rollerblade and play tennis with our boys. So many memories of her cheeky, smiley, happy face as I walked down those streets. But every time I stepped out in front of a bus at a pedestrian crossing, I was crudely reminded of how all those loving memories came to a violent end.

My attempts at reasoning and trying to understand why Charlotte was killed led me to a dead end. God was silent and my faith gave me no answers. My mind was still plagued by the image of Charlotte's lifeless face. There wasn't a day that went past when I would pray and believe that God would protect my family and no harm would come to them. Maybe sometimes I prayed out of fear rather than faith which contradict each other but still motivated me to pray. My reality now is that harm has made a vicious impact on my family and my prayers seemed to have fallen on deaf ears.

I had to find a way to silence the voices in my head that told me my faith was unreal. Had I been deceived? Was there any hope at all? This reminded me of when I used to fight in gangs as a teenager. Once I was surrounded, outnumbered by a hungry pack of wolves waiting to pounce on me. I could choose to curl up in a ball and let my enemies kick the living daylights out of me, or I could fight like a wild animal kicking and screaming in the desperate hope that it would be enough to scare my enemies away. Fortunately for me the latter worked and they ran away.

I felt like that again, except this time my faith was backed against the wall fighting for survival. Do I give up my faith or could I somehow turn this around and make this evil mockery flee in retreat? I felt surrounded by darkness. This was where my faith was going to stand or fall. My faith could not answer the question of why my daughter had been killed. I couldn't control what had happened, but I could control the way I responded. The Gospel message is about bringing life out of death. My God had not forsaken me. This was about standing in the face of adversity, going toe to toe, face to face with evil personified and proclaiming, "No, this is not your time to steal, kill and destroy my soul. But out of the ashes of death, my faith will rise again."

My faith teaches me that as long as I have breath in me, I do have a meaningful purpose on this earth. I can turn my tragedy into hope. I can start a foundation in honour of Charlotte. Her memory will live on in the lives of other young people by helping them realise their potential in the performing arts. This makes my faith all the more intentional, both personally and publicly. I can make a spectacle of my daughter's meaningless death. I can turn her tragic story from hopelessness and despair into one of hope and faith, delivering a true story of redemption.

The week after Charlotte's memorial I received a phone call from the *Billy Elliot* productions office. The director of the show was so moved by the service at Charlotte's memorial and by the words I had spoken, 'I will never forget my gorgeous daughter and I'm gonna make sure you don't either...'

He felt really challenged by those words and wanted to make sure that people would never forget who Charlotte was and what she meant to the *Billy Elliot* show. On April 19,

2011, the *Billy Elliot* show was going to dedicate this one night as a tribute to Charlotte. I was really taken by surprise and astonished at how fast this tribute show was organised, only sixteen days after Charlotte's memorial.

Before I had even taken account of where I was and what I was doing, I found myself standing outside the Victoria Palace theatre, staring up at the *Billy Elliot* sign. I had been given sixty free tickets for my family and friends to attend. Along with the tickets they had printed a special programme:

A performance for Charlotte. On Thursday, March 17, 2011, Charlotte Leatherbarrow, one of our Ballet Girls, was tragically killed in a road accident. Tonight's performance is dedicated to Charlotte and her contribution *to Billy Elliot the Musical*. Charlotte's parents have set up the Charlotte Leatherbarrow Foundation which will assist other parents who struggle to pay for dance classes for their children. The Foundation's purpose is to enable young and gifted performers to fulfil their potential. *Billy Elliot the Musical* is proud to support the Foundation and after tonight's performance we will be making a collection on its behalf. We would be incredibly grateful if you would help us fill the buckets that the cast will be holding at all the exits of the theatre. Any donation, large or small, is very welcome. The New York, Toronto and US Tour productions of *Billy Elliot the Musical* will also be dedicating Tuesday, April 19, as a Performance for Charlotte and will be making collections for the Foundation.

As I sat down with my family to watch a special performance that night, the atmosphere was electric, both on and off the stage. Of course, when it came to the parts Charlotte would have performed, all I could see was the joy and colour of her when I'd last seen her lighting up the stage on Christmas Eve.

The cast gave a very moving performance for Charlotte, and then at the end one of the cast members, Alan Bradshaw, came onto the stage and spoke this message:

"One month ago Charlotte Leatherbarrow, one of our Ballet Girls, was tragically involved in a fatal accident in Herne Hill whilst on her way to dance class. In my role as Children's Dance Captain I spend hours rehearsing with our Ballet Girls, and I cannot express how much of a pleasure and privilege it was to teach and work with such a special girl. She came to each rehearsal with a fantastic smile on her face and such admirable determination. Added to her natural talent this made for a generous and dedicated performer. Not only that, but Charlotte was a good friend to the other girls and an inspiration to us all, and a joy to have as part of our production. So tonight is very much a celebration. Not just here in London but also on our productions in New York and Toronto we have dedicated two consecutive performances to honouring Charlotte, her wonderful portrayal of Sharon Percy, and her huge contribution to the show. We all know how much Charlotte loved being on the stage and her parents Karen and Neil found a poem she had written about her experiences here with us at *Billy Elliot*."

Connor, who played Michael in the show, stepped forward to recite Charlotte's poem:

The stage lights beaming in your face
The tingle in your tummy, the buzz in your feet
The applause, your everlasting smile.
The joy, inside you just can't hide
The friends, family greet you in joy,
But your body is sleepy; your eyes are gloomy,
Your feet are droopy.
I put my head on my pillow and rest my
Sleepy body and my gloomy eyes,
And my droopy feet and all that buzz,
Of excitement will rest for another night...

The audience was silent; I couldn't look around to see the expressions on people's faces. I was just trying to hold myself together. Alan continued his speech:

"Karen and Neil have set up the Charlotte Leatherbarrow Foundation, which is for brilliant youngsters of individual character and distinct personality. It's about giving those aged eight to sixteen from ordinary backgrounds access to the kind of training which most of us here were lucky enough to get. Also, importantly, it will make sure that the name Charlotte Leatherbarrow lives on as it should. So as you leave the theatre this evening, members of the cast will be at the exits with buckets, and we invite you to contribute as much or as little as you can. All is much appreciated and will go to such a wonderful cause so other youngsters may reach their dreams as Charlotte did. Thank you for being part of our celebration. Goodnight."

The audience filed out of the theatre to the noise of coins dropping into plastic buckets. I walked out to the bar area to get a cold drink with my family in tow. We were told that after people had left, we would go back into the theatre with our friends for another tribute from the cast of the show. Karen and I were ushered to the front to sit down while the *Billy Elliot* choreographer and company manager stood up on stage to convey a very personal and touching tribute to Charlotte.

This was so overwhelming and seemed so surreal that this huge tribute was all in respect of our daughter and for setting up her foundation. Karen and I were invited up on stage to give a final tribute. I can't remember what Karen or I said that night, it was all such a blur. I could only think to express gratitude to everyone who had been involved in such an undertaking and ended by saying, "I'm on a mission from God now to go out and find those new young Billy Elliots and help give them the same opportunities my daughter had."

My hands were shaking nervously as I finished and our friends clapped enthusiastically as we left the stage. This felt so unreal as if I were having an out-of-body experience watching someone else's life. My mind was deceiving me; this was all just a bad dream and I would wake up soon. Except this was all too real and I would never wake up. At least I felt I had a purpose and one that I could carry on for the rest of my life.

A few days after the tribute, I received an email from the director of productions informing me of how much was raised on the night. The London collection from the audience raised just over £2,600, breaking all *Billy Elliot* fundraising records, more than double the usual amount collected on a single night. In addition to the collection, they raised at least another £3,000 from the UK cast, company, creative team and producers. Working Title was going to be giving £5,000, and, on top of all that, Sir Elton John and David Furnish were also giving £5,000. The American and Canadian companies sent these messages:

The Broadway production raised over $5,100 for 'A Performance for Charlotte' – more than double our average daily collection during the Broadway Cares/Equity Fights AIDS fundraising campaign and a high number for our theatre. Greg Jbara gave a very moving speech at the end of the performance, including a reading of Charlotte's poem. It was incredibly moving and we're thankful the large spring break audiences could contribute. Our signed window cards, autographed playbills and specialty made fundraising buttons all sold well, in addition to cash donations. As you know, Broadway Cares/EFA have agreed to donate one hundred percent of the proceeds from 'A Performance for Charlotte' directly to her foundation. We are extremely grateful to them and The Shubert Organization for their unwavering support of this special night. Finally, our Ballet Girls sent handwritten cards, paintings, and notes directly to both Charlotte's family and the London Ballet Girls to offer their condolences, love, and support. We heard today from David Massey that these notes were incorporated into a memory book made in her honor and presented to her family last night, so they are extremely honored to play a part in honoring Charlotte.

We are very pleased to report that *Billy* Toronto has raised over $7,700 for the Charlotte Leatherbarrow Foundation... and counting! Last night at the 'Performance for Charlotte', we collected bucket donations, sold autographed special edition posters, sold Polaroid photos with Billy and Michael, and auctioned off a 'Billy Elliot Experience' for the winning bidder to come back and see the show again, spend some time with the cast, and do a walk-on in one of the scenes. I say 'still counting' because we are still selling the posters, and many people in the building indicated that they will be making additional donations in the coming days. So, we will give you a full report once we have our grand total, but wanted to share this news. Kate Hennig's words at the end were a lovely tribute to Charlotte and we were all so honored to be a part of this night.

Our US Tour collection for Charlotte Leatherbarrow last night was our single highest collection by far, bringing in $6,551. We were so pleased to be able to support this.

Altogether the combined shows raised just under £30,000, and to finish it off Charlotte's name would be written in the official London *Billy Elliot* programme for as long as the show continued. I couldn't have asked for a better start to setting up the foundation. I am so grateful to everyone involved with *Billy Elliot*.

Soon after the *Billy Elliot* tribute one of Charlotte's team from the show, Sophia, and her mum made contact with me.

They told me how they were going to organise a performance called 'Let the Light Shine On' on June 2, 2011. This was going to include most of the Ballet Girls team from *Billy Elliot* and more of Sophia's friends. They were all going to perform dance solos and duets and invite their family and friends to buy tickets and watch them perform especially in honour of Charlotte. The final performance would be all of them doing the tap finale from *Billy Elliot*.

Karen and I attended the show and it proved a real success. As hard as it was watching Charlotte's friends perform without her, we were very moved by their compassion to dance for her and how much pleasure it gave them. We stood up at the end to speak on behalf of Charlotte and the Foundation. We thanked all the performers and people working behind the scenes to make this event happen. Karen found it difficult not to cry while thanking everyone. I stood next to her and thought to myself this was something I would probably have to get used to doing, especially as I was going to try and raise more money for Charlotte's foundation.

They raised just over £1,600 on the night and enjoyed doing it so much they wanted to do another show around the same time in 2012. I began to realise that starting her foundation meant leaving her life behind as much as I would try to relive it. I could only build on my memories of her and those that wanted to remember her with me.

Our home in Herne Hill was empty without the life of Charlotte filling it and a daily reminder of how we could not fill the void that she had left behind. Sometimes, when I would be working from home, sitting at my desk, I would see Charlotte when she came home from school, which was only two hundred metres down the road. She would always press her face against the rose-coloured stained glass of the front door and stare inside. I often caught myself staring back at the front door around three thirty every afternoon, still waiting to see if Charlotte's face would by some miracle appear through the window.

Driving Jason to school every morning, I would try to avoid going down Herne Hill past the scene of the accident, although sometimes it was unavoidable. These constant reminders would be just another stab in the heart, another agonising memory of my loss. Of course people were going about their daily lives, oblivious to our tragedy, walking past the lamp post which for weeks had flowers tied around it as a remembrance to Charlotte. Like watching the sun go down after a long day, I was slowly realising that our life in Herne Hill and Dulwich was coming to an end. We needed to start to build a new life without Charlotte.

Some dear friends of my family had already offered their second home for us to move into. The house was situated close to the river Thames in leafy Putney, South West London, an area that had no familiarity with Charlotte. This was a place where we could start to build an alternate life. Our life in South East London had become a memorial to Charlotte and our hopes and dreams of a complete family had died with her. If we were going to survive, we needed to start again. It was excruciatingly painful to leave behind all the memories that made us so happy and yet, at the same time, were tearing us apart inside.

We had to leave behind all that we could in order to build a future with what was left of our family. This was not healing. This was carrying on, regardless of the pain we faced. The loss of Charlotte was not something we would ever get over. It is more a learning to live without and starting to build again with what we have left. Bringing life out of Charlotte's death doesn't mean we stay in the same place. We move on. It is a journey going forwards and not back. Putney was to become our new home for now. Living with change is never easy, but a process of transition, a perpetual motion that will always be a part of our lives.

It was dawning on me that I was not designed to cope with death or the loss of love. It is agony. I was meant to live in a world free from the constraints of this life. Surely death was not final but only the beginning of a new life in an eternal home where I hoped Charlotte was living now. Only faith could give me the eyes to see and grace to grant me the patience to wait.

We left packing up Charlotte's room until last. We gave away some of her things and bedroom furniture and then carefully boxed up the rest of her belongings to take to our new home. On the final day of moving out, I walked into her room and collapsed on the bare floor, staring at the emptiness. I thought of how this was a perfect reflection of my state of mind. I had lived and moved to many different places and countries in my lifetime, but no journey was as vast as the one I was about to embark on. Even though the journey was only about ten miles away, it was the crossing of an ocean to me.

# Chapter 7
## Out of Control

At least my mum was happy to have me back in her life. I pleaded with her not to make me start another new school and she agreed, giving me a six month respite. I found myself staring out of the bedroom window again. I was fifteen, introverted, a recluse. I didn't even venture outside of the house. The large intake of valium had no effect and my mother's own drug addiction was destroying her third marriage. When she could not get enough of her sedative, she was unbearable to be around. Her moods were very dark and the language she used was enough to emasculate any man.

Gerry was a jealous man and resented the time I was spending at home with his new wife. This led to a violent climax when Gerry put his fist through a door and fortunately not in my mum's face or mine. I stared at hopelessness again, this time feeling like quicksand was pulling me down and I didn't know what to hold onto. I felt depressed about my life. Had I hit rock bottom? I didn't know. During my absence from school I had plenty of time to reflect over the years of turbulence and upheaval. I could count ten different homes and around ten new schools by the time I reached my fifteenth birthday.

Most of my school life was during the 1970s, a time when there was a major change from the old grammar school system to the modern comprehensive. Most of the schools I had attended up and down the country were still suffering from a hangover of Victorian discipline. And I never seemed to like school. My earliest memory of starting at primary school was running away on the first day. At my second primary school in Cornwall the headmaster was convicted for physically abusing the children. I remember being petrified of the man when I sat in class doing a spelling test. For every word I spelt incorrectly, I would receive a whack on my knuckles with a wooden ruler. Consequently, by the time I had finished that school at the age of six, my knuckles were made of leather.

It's not just the pain or intimidation you remember but the humiliation you feel for looking a fool in front of your classmates. The two schools I attended in Wales still employed corporal punishment, which meant the head teacher used a leather whip for disciplining unruly children like me. In retrospect, having a grown man tell an eight-year-old child to pull his pants down and bend over while he whipped you with six of his best still disturbs me today. There was another eccentric Welsh teacher who found a way of disciplining his students in front of the class by making them bend over while he literally kicked them up the backside.

At Minehead Middle School, my physical education teacher, who like most other physical education teachers I had, really fancied himself and seemed to enjoy taking his frustration out on his unknowing students. One time in the changing rooms I started whistling the Great Escape theme tune. I was conducting the rest of the class when the teacher walked in behind me. He grabbed me by my hair and dragged me into his office. He told me never to whistle in his lessons again, before instructing me to take down my pants. Then he took his leather shoe and gave me six of his best across my bare backside. That really hurt too.

At my last school in West Somerset my wood and metal work teacher was a big six foot eight inch hairy giant. He rode into school on his Harley Davidson motorbike every day. A very intimidating character to say the least, he took great pleasure in showing up his lesser students. Whenever I made a mistake with my work, which happened frequently, he would literally pick me up by my feet and bang my head on the side of the wooden bench.

"What's a dovetail joint, idiot?" he would say, menacingly.

"Uh, I don't know, sir," would be my feeble reply.

Bang went my head on the side of the bench. Boy, did I hate his lessons, but I had my revenge when he was giving us a practical demonstration of the circular saw and, just for one second, took his eyes off the piece of wood he was cutting. He severed the top of his thumb and how sweet his cry of pain sounded that day.

Then there was my English teacher, an attractive twenty-two year old woman who took a fancy to teenage boys, including yours truly. She used to enjoy teasing us whenever she would bend over to mark our work and reveal a little too much of her cleavage. During one lesson we all had our heads down busily writing some essay. She came up to me and indiscreetly rubbed her genitals over my hand on the side of the desk. Smiling, she wrote a note on my book, 'see me afterwards', and then sauntered back to her desk at the front of the class.

I sat there in shock for the rest of the lesson, unable to complete my work. Again, I felt like I was reading about some sexual fantasy made up in a porn magazine, except this was for real. I never stayed to find out what my English teacher was going to propose and I always avoided being on my own with her. For some reason I thought the whole idea of getting intimately involved with a teacher was crazy. I think my rational judgement got the better of me and not my raging hormones. What she was thinking, I will never know. Even though these experiences will be forever engraved on my memory, not all my teachers were sadistic and perverted.

My memory of the headmaster at Riverside Junior School in Hullbridge, Essex was a good one. I'll always remember him for being fair and just but above all kind to me during my turbulent time there. He would often ask me how things were at home and always make time to listen. Also my history teacher at the West Somerset School was inspirational. I used to love listening to his own personal stories about the Second World War and they helped develop my love for the subject. We were studying about the Nuremberg Trials of 1946, when the Allies were holding all the remaining Nazi officers accountable for crimes against humanity.

My history teacher would tell us about his own experience of being an army guard during the trials. He would make us laugh when he told us about Hermann Goering, the commander of the Luftwaffe, and how he loved wearing his white suits and flirting with the lawyers in the courtroom because he was gay. Finally, there was my sports coach who was an ex-parachute regiment soldier, inspiring me to take up fitness training as a daily part of my life. He personified the typical army 'never say die' attitude even when we were snowed in and the school was closed. My coach still turned up, having just jogged through the heavy snow. I always remembered the good teachers and not just the bad ones.

As I reflected back on my school days during this time of solitude, a lasting impression of the resilience of children formed in my mind. Every time I was knocked down, I would always bounce back again. At each new school I attended I would always find my way to become a popular member of the class. Being the 'new kid on the block' had its advantages as well as disadvantages. At first you were a novelty, and then later on I had to work hard at gaining a new friend's trust. Just when I had established my place in the class, I moved again and the story would repeat itself.

By now the strain was obvious. Each move cemented a fear and hatred of the education system to the point where I just couldn't face the ordeal of another new school. Where did my strength come from? What gave me hope that the grass is always greener on the other side? Was it a false hope that was leading me down a path with no certainty? What is it about macho men? They come across with such bravado, they love to dominate, and yet they feel so easily threatened and insecure.

My first stepfather, Michael, was definitely a macho man. Although how he felt threatened by a ten-year-old boy I don't know. What would make a man beat or physically intimidate a boy is beyond me. He certainly didn't like my influence over my mother and I assumed his drunken state of mind contributed to his irrational behaviour. When he used to knock me to the ground, I would defy him by standing up again. This same action would continue over and over until I learnt, like an obedient dog, that it was better to stay down than be beaten again. But on other occasions I would still challenge him even though I was just a young boy fighting against a grown man.

Out of this abusive relationship there, a fighter, was rising up in me, determined that a man like him would never keep me down. This was the kind of strength I could draw from that helped me face my fears. I dug deep and found some inner strength that helped me make a decision. What I was experiencing now at the age of fifteen was no worse than what I had experienced as a young boy during my mother's marriage to Michael. I believed by accepting my past I could gain the strength to help me live in the present and face the future with some certainty. I really needed to rally all the courage I could find to face going back to another school.

Then I remembered the time when I was eight years old and lived in the Lake District. My parents were delving into the world of spiritualism and invited a spirit medium into the house to hold regular séance-like meetings. One night I participated in a séance and consequently fell into a trance. All I could remember was falling down, endlessly, into a dark hole. Meanwhile, my body convulsed and writhed on the floor. My father panicked and shook me out of the trance. This led to consistent nightmares and physical manifestations causing broken and sleepless nights for the next eight years. The only relief would be a drug-induced sleep and even that didn't always work.

Life at home in Grange, a little village just outside of Keswick, felt dark and gloomy, a remarkable contrast to the beauty of the surrounding countryside. My brother and I decided, out of our own volition, to join a youth club run by the local church. The youth leaders were very warm and friendly. I remember constantly trying to seek their attention. Like metal to a magnet, I was drawn to these people.

Then an event occurred that took me completely by surprise. Our church organised a trip to go and see *Come Together,* a hippy musical born out of the Jesus People revolution in the late '60s that mixed the Gospel message with country rock music. I loved it. The theatre was filled with an atmosphere I had never experienced before. Hundreds of people were jumping, dancing and happy, in love with this Jesus, the central character in this musical extravaganza. Catchy songs and a lively narrative kept me wanting more and longing for the evening to never come to an end.

There was a passion radiating from these people that was infectious. I felt my heart change that night. What a contrast this was compared to my frightening experience in the séance. It was almost as if there was a battle between light and darkness fighting for control of my life. I lived on the edge of the local council housing estate and I used to visit a boy called Ian who lived in a typical two-up two-down brick house on the estate. He came from a large Catholic family of seven children. His father was unemployed and his mother was struggling to raise their children on a minimal income.

I'll never forget the day I first visited his home. I walked through their front door and had to walk straight out again, immediately vomiting on their doorstep because of the stench that radiated from the house. I had never smelt anything like it before. I made up an excuse that I wasn't feeling well as I was too embarrassed to tell them what their home smelt like. When I returned home, my mum stripped my clothes off and washed them straight away. I had never experienced poverty to this extreme before in England and have witnessed none like it since.

At my local junior school, Ian was rejected and ridiculed daily. He smelt so bad that nobody wanted to sit next to him in class. There were gangs of kids that wandered the streets at night looking for trouble, armed with bangers (loud fireworks). One evening Ian was confronted by a gang who threw some bangers at him and one of them hit Ian in the face, permanently blinding him in one eye. I had decided to be friends with Ian, in fact his only friend, and often stood up for him against the rest of the school. This led to the school treating me with the same ridicule and torment to which Ian had been subjected.

I remembered all the mockery, fights, spitting in my face and general provocation and how it seemed to fall off me like water off a duck's back. With my newfound compassion I had an absolute conviction that I was doing the right thing in defending my friend Ian. This was a defining moment in my life, one that would motivate my belief in standing up for the poor, marginalised, and social outcasts that I lived and worked with in the years ahead. This was formative to my belief in social justice and shaped my value of compassion in life. A belief that was not just driven by logic that rationalizes everything but by a passion in my guts that takes action.

I believe a drop of hope can overcome an ocean of hopelessness. That's what the Gospel musical meant for me. It was like a burst of light and energy that blew away the fear and darkness. This experience was to be a lasting memory, one that gave me an injection of hope to help me through the hard times to come. In the spring of 1982 I told my mum I was ready to go back to school. Maylandsea was a quiet riverside village in the Dengie Peninsula on the east coast. If you followed the river upstream for a few miles, there was Maldon town where my next and final school was going to be, the Plume Upper School.

Summoning the courage to go back to school was one thing, but there was also a pool of chaotic energy that I couldn't contain any longer. My return to school appeared to ignite this flammable fuel inside me. On the one hand, I was hungry to learn, I wanted to be inspired. On the other hand I not only disrupted the class by playing the court jester but I would lash out like an angry lion let out of its cage if a teacher dared to lay a finger on me.

During the summer break, my mum and Gerry announced we were moving house again. Our new home was going to be my grandparents' house in Chelmsford, roughly half an hour's car journey from my school. My grandmother had joined a religious cult and moved into a community house in Aylesbury about seventy miles away. She had kindly offered her home for us to live in and pay rent.

I couldn't believe my ears, and the thought of changing schools again would have driven me over the edge of my sanity. I had been suspended from school already for my disruptive behaviour. My mum's solution was to start over at another school so I could have a clean break. I stubbornly refused, so they came up with a good compromise. They were going to buy me a motorbike for my sixteenth birthday so I could make my own way to school.

My black Yamaha RD50 was my ride to freedom. I was born to be wild every morning between eight and nine, cruising down the A414 to Maldon. To pay for my freedom, I took a job at the local Kentucky Fried Chicken takeaway. I worked two to three nights a week and, because of my age, I was underpaid, earning only eighty pence an hour. That was bad even for the early '80s. My new biker image epitomized my 'punk' attitude and sheer determination to discover my independence. With a black helmet, or 'lid' as my fellow biker mates called it, a black Yamaha leather jacket, and black steel toe capped boots, I was definitely too cool for school.

I even bought a new 'bore' kit and exhaust pipe for my bike that essentially turned it into a 65cc engine instead of a 50cc. This meant I could reach a top speed of fifty miles per hour and outrun any motorbike or scooter at school. Together with my friend Chippy, we would terrorize the town centre, burning up and down the high street, trying to impress the girls who were too preoccupied with window-shopping for something new. Then, one day, I tried to pull a wheelie by the mini roundabout at the top of the high street, parading my showmanship for all to see. I was totally oblivious to the car coming from my right, and, slamming into the side of it, I was knocked clean off my bike.

I lay on the ground stunned and looked up at two nuns bending down with their crucifixes waving round their necks. They politely enquired after my well-being but my ego was too bruised to accept their kindness. I quickly exchanged details, straightened out my bent handlebars, jumped on my bike, and rode off with my engine spluttering and stammering. I revved my engine as loud as I could to try and drown out the mocking crowd that had gathered around us. I fled the comical scene wishing the day would end sooner rather than later.

Tyler was the kind of person you could confide in. He was a good listener and a faithful friend. He fashioned himself on Bob Dylan and introduced me to great music like The Rolling Stones, Led Zeppelin and many more rock legends. He also helped kick-start my love for playing drums. I had managed to save some money by the summer of 1983, so I went out and bought my first drum kit. A sparkly silver Premier four-piece kit, it didn't sound very good, but it was my first so I loved it. One of my favourite bands topped the charts that summer with a hit that would go down as one the best pop rock songs ever, 'Every Breath You Take' by The Police. And it was a good song for me to practise along to.

Tyler also helped me to chill out and stop being such an angry punk. We would sit and listen to Pink Floyd while smoking 'heavenly blues'. I didn't know what was in it but the substance certainly had a hypnotic and calming effect. My new sense of inner peace didn't last very long though. At one of our friend's wild parties I found my girlfriend in a room kissing another guy. The anger welled up inside me again. With spontaneous rage I attacked my two-timing girlfriend and her new one-night stand. My fists flying relentlessly, I couldn't control my anger from spilling over. The violence only ended when friends pulled me away from them and threw me out of the party.

I stormed off on my motorbike. Fortunately, adrenaline had kicked in with a sobering effect, which enabled me to ride my bike without crashing. When I reached home, I was confronted by my mother and Gerry having another fight. I told him to leave her alone. He just knocked me out of the way and drove off in his car. My mum had been slapped around a bit but wasn't badly bruised. She was doped up with valium and wasn't making any sense so I just put her to bed. I collapsed in the lounge, put my headphones on to shut out the world and lose myself in the music. 'King of Pain' by The Police came on with its lyrics about a little black spot on the sun today being the same old thing as yesterday.

My thoughts were sobering. No matter how hard I was trying to gain my independence, the past kept coming back to haunt me, a deliberate reminder of what was really going on inside, as if a darkness was trying to cover up the light. I was also confronted with my own hypocrisy. I was trying to change my life, be a better person than my so-called father figures, and yet here I was beating a girl with my fists just like my stepfather. I was becoming what I hated, even though the rebel in me wanted to change. My life seemed to be spinning out of control and all I could do was drown my self-loathing in the bottom of a whiskey bottle.

# Chapter 8
## Freefall

September 2011, six months had passed. Karen and I sat inside a small room at Brixton Police Station. The sun was shining through the window, but everything felt dark. Our family liaison officer gave us a cup of water while the two detectives from the crash investigation team sat opposite us. The leader of the team, a tall, thin, grey-haired gentleman, did most of the talking. He was there to explain how and why Charlotte was killed. He started off by thanking Karen for giving such an honest account in her statement of what happened on the night of March 17.

He made a point of saying that most statements taken from witnesses are often exaggerated. Their main witness apart from Karen was a lady doctor who was sitting four cars behind ours. Due to her profession, she gave the most matter of fact account of what she had witnessed. He went on to explain that the head of the investigation team was a scientific expert on fatal collisions such as this. They called them 'raw deaths' and his opinion was the most significant. The detail was meticulous and explicit. They had judged that at the moment of impact, Charlotte had sped up to seven miles an hour in just one metre. The bus was travelling at sixteen miles an hour at the moment of impact. This gave the driver less than a second to react before the collision.

As I listened to the officer's long, drawn-out conclusion, I felt hopelessly blind and dumb. I could not be given the satisfaction of knowing why Charlotte was killed the way she was. Science could not explain it, my faith could not justify it, and nobody could tell me why. Just when you want the truth to be black and white, it turns out to be grey. I wanted to jump up from my seat and scream with frustration. My daughter's death was left to random chance?

It was random that Charlotte's head took the full force of the bus's impact. It was random that she fell to the other side of the bus as she was sucked under by the momentum of the bus. It was random that her head was caught between the axle and the wheel of the bus. So if the impact hadn't killed her, being crushed underneath the bus did. This moment of madness took just a few seconds to end Charlotte's life. Her injuries were all to her head and face and there was not a mark on her body or legs. Everything that could have gone wrong went wrong and all because her life was left to random chance?

My wound was not only deep, there was no closure, no reconciliation in this scientific conclusion, no rational reason. God again was silent; my faith was in free fall and I could find no solid ground to tread. I had to be brave in order to live outside of a world I so desperately wanted to be black and white. In a scientific world everything is explainable, everything is understandable and there are always answers to our questions. We can put them in a nice little box and file it away. Except now my world was in chaos. There was no truth or explanation as to why Charlotte died the way she did.

Obviously, you don't run out in front of a travelling bus. Although, how many of us have made mistakes crossing a busy road when nothing incidental happens, no harm is done? There was no reason why the collision unfolded the way it did. If Charlotte had been hit by a car doing the same speed her body would have compensated and she most certainly would have lived. Colliding with a bus was like being hit by a ten ton moving brick wall. I wanted to know the truth but the truth was both brutal and merciless.

Our scientific experts tell us that for every cause there is an effect, for every action there is a reaction. This makes the world controllable, predictable, there is always certainty. But the loss of my daughter and the randomness of her accident inform me of a reality that is so uncertain. My grief informs me that I live in a world that is not always explicable or understandable. Science cannot give me the answers I seek.

I was so tempted to blame someone or something. I wanted to be able to justify my daughter's death to find some kind of meaning. I needed to close the door on such a dark chapter in my life but I had no answers, no comprehension. This was like a gaping wound that could not be healed. How cruel and unforgiving life could be. The only crude answer we had was the coroner's conclusion from his inquest, 'cause of death – accidental'.

Karen and I were invited to attend the court case that was held shortly after my birthday. It took months for the crash investigation team and the coroner to assemble all the details of Charlotte's fatal collision. All I had to show for it at the end was a death certificate which I needed to collect from the Register of Births and Deaths at the local town hall.

There I was, sitting in the registry office filling out a form for Charlotte, in one hand her birth certificate and the other her death certificate. A Chinese lady came and sat down beside me, looking bewildered. She turned to me and in her broken English asked me to help her fill out a form registering the birth of her daughter. At that moment I felt like the floodgates were going to burst open. My eyes welled up with tears. I put my head down trying to hide them, holding back all those beautiful years I had known my daughter. How surreal can life get?

During those last few months everybody else around us had resumed their normal everyday lives with their families. This kind of normality had come to an abrupt halt for us. Without Charlotte, our lives were so empty. From waking in the morning to going to bed at night, Charlotte was absent and never coming back. I had not realised how I had taken my family life for granted, a life that was so certain and was now so fragile. Our grief seemed to drag us down inside a deep, dark hole where nobody would want to venture. We were living in a different time zone, out of sync with the rest of the world, falling.

I'm going to show you a letter now that someone wrote to us shortly after Charlotte's accident. Both Karen and I were so grateful for how she managed to write this, her words really reached out to us at the time and still do.

Dear Karen and Neil, I was so sorry to have only learnt this weekend about Charlotte and wanted to write to you both to say how devastated I feel for you and your family, and to send my utmost sympathy. My instant reaction was to reach out and want to offer something to you both…but what…sympathy…condolences? Immediately one is left retracting, thinking…what can I say? What difference can anything make that I offer? I don't know… but I will try, and hope that this letter is better than not writing anything at all. I don't know if you remember me, my two daughters Rosa and Tilly were at the dance school for several years before finishing a couple of years back. I will always remember Charlotte – she was hard not to notice. The prettiest and the brightest of the bunch, I always envied her hair! Karen we didn't talk that much, but I always knew you as Charlotte's mum. A name and an honour no doubt you will wear with pride. I wasn't aware that she was dancing in Billy Elliot, but it didn't surprise me. There were some dancers who simply had that special quality and even though I am not a dancer, and couldn't tell a plié from a pas de deux…Charlotte was always magical to watch. It has been ten years since I lost my own little boy. He was nearly six. He had leukaemia since the age of one and had relapsed three years into the treatment. I remember talking to the father of a boy who had died eighteen months earlier, and he told me that the second year was worse than the first. How could that be? I remember screaming inwardly and thinking nothing could be worse… nothing! But I think he meant that, after getting through the first year he had hoped that the following year would be easier and because it wasn't...it seemed worse. I'm glad he told me that because after that I didn't expect it to be better. Although part of you thinks that if you have managed to get through one day...one month... one year... then you know you can make it through another. What can I say... ten years on... is that when I feel the pain it never changes. I hurt now as much as I ever did. But the time in between the pain lengthens, and I am able to spend more and more of my day just doing everyday things without being drowned in grief. I liken it to floating on a raft. I can feel the sun, and see the shore, and everything looks fine. But I only have to dip my head for one second, and my face is staring into the abyss in a dark ocean where I am unable to breathe. My life is about learning how to keep lifting my head above the water. And so I cry into that ocean... I cry for me... I cry for you... I cry for all the parents who have ever lost children. And I send you both an imaginary raft that you can reach out for, and climb onto whenever you feel you are drowning...

In this time of free fall, I felt I had nothing to hold onto. When my wound was the deepest, it is profound words like this that bring great comfort. It is as if someone is reaching out to you with an olive branch of hope or a raft in an ocean of grief. Thank you, Sara. We always talk about Charlotte around meal times to keep her alive and fresh in our minds. We laugh and cry as we remember her, painful and comforting at the same time. The truth slowly dawns on us, whether we like it or not, we have to learn to let her go.

Psychologists say that the grief of losing a child is like no other because it upsets the natural order of life. This makes me feel like I am living in an alternate reality. The history and course of my family's life has been permanently changed. All I have left of Charlotte is a collection of memories, pictures and personal belongings. I guess I should be grateful for that but it is the physical senses that I miss the most. We have three locks of her hair left kept in purple pouches. These are the last physical remains we have of Charlotte.

We have so many personal belongings of hers and we have given so much away to her friends for keepsakes. Fortunately, with today's technology, we have hundreds of photos and video footage of Charlotte from the time when she was born right up until the time she died. I will never lose what she looked and sounded like. I have lost the sense of smell. It's not something I really thought about until she was gone. She had such a distinct smell about her, her clothes, her hair, and her skin. The aroma that my daughter created around me vanished too quickly.

The most obvious sense I lost, of course, was to touch, to hold her close; Daddy was always the one she played silly games with. I was the one who always carried her on my back up to her bedroom at night. These times I will never be able to revive. The pain of loss is unbearable. She is my first thought in the morning and my last thoughts at night. I think about her every day. I feel robbed and my anger consumes me some days but I don't want to hurt anybody so I go to the gym. Tears mixed with sweat, I take my anger out on exercise, pushing myself to exhaustion.

Before Charlotte's death, I never had the chance to say any last words or do anything. Even if I knew she was going to die, I had no way of preparing myself. I would have liked to have spent one more day with her just to say goodbye, but I couldn't. Charlotte didn't just die, she was killed. I have avoided happy-clapping churches because I don't relate to this kind of reality. I don't need Christians who want to try and fix me or say something spiritual that makes sense of it all when nothing can.

"God will heal you in time," they say.

I know they are well-meaning people, but it doesn't really help. How can I really be healed? The only thing that could possibly heal me is the impossible, to bring my daughter back from the dead, even if it was just for a moment. If a soldier came back from a tour of duty having been injured by a land mine and lost their leg, you wouldn't say to them, 'Don't worry, in time you'll heal and grow another one!' That would be stupid. The soldier will have to learn to live without that leg and build a different life. In the same way, now I've lost my daughter I will have to learn to live without her and forge an alternate life for myself and my family.

"I like to think it was Charlotte's time."

"Charlotte was too good for this world."

"Did you do something bad to deserve this?"

These are all explanations that try to justify, rationalize or defend our beliefs. They try to bring closure and give some possible meaning to such a tragedy. Do bad things only happen to bad people? Why couldn't Charlotte continue to make such a difference in this world? Charlotte was meant to die at the age of twelve and in such a horrific way? None of

114

these answers or questions could give me rest or peace. As for trying to find answers for why tragedies like this happen, sometimes there are none. As Christians we sometimes try to fit the world and God inside a box, but life just doesn't work that way. I believe God lives outside the box and so can we.

Something else I have learnt during this time of free fall is that many men are useless at dealing with grief and handling deep emotion. For every fifty messages Karen received from her female friends, I might have received one or two from my male counterparts. Even then the message would say, "I'm always here for you mate. Just give me a call," just when you need them to call you and reach out to you. I believe that friends should be there to share in the good times as well as the bad. But some of my friends could not be there for me. They could not talk or listen. They felt too awkward to even be around me. I would go out for coffee or a drink with them and some would want to try to fix me. Of course, they can't and when they discovered this, they would just tell me to get some counselling. All I needed was for them to have a listening ear. Listening seems to be a lost art these days, even when it is one of our deepest needs. This hurt me because I felt I couldn't share the real me and the pain that was now a part of my life.

I believe in taking risks to share the painful times because our relationships are all the richer and fuller for it. Surely this should bring us closer and forge a stronger bond between friends? By burying, denying or ignoring our pain we don't allow people or give them the freedom to know us for who we really are. Instead, I felt rejected by friends denying me the right to share the real me and that forged a gap between us. Despite my disappointment, I do have a couple of friends who reach out to me, even if one of them is my counsellor.

Every memorable date in the calendar became a milestone in my journey with grief, and with Christmas looming, it felt like a mountain to ascend. The last Christmas we spent together with my family was probably the best. Charlotte was performing in a matinee show of *Billy Elliot* on Christmas Eve. I felt very proud and then we all went out to have Christmas dinner at Café Rouge. It was a perfect day, but now we had to anticipate spending the next Christmas without her.

I used to sneak into my kids' bedrooms on Christmas Eve to watch them sleeping soundly before the excitement of opening presents the next day. When Charlotte was little, she would sleep with her bottom sticking up in the air and I would tuck her in under her bed covers. Now all I could do was stare at the end of my bed where a plastic urn was tucked away underneath with my daughter's ashes inside. This may seem strange to some people but we just wanted to keep her close. The difference in expectation at Christmastime couldn't be more extreme.

At this stage, my grief still felt like it was dragging me down. I was falling and didn't know when I was going to hit rock bottom. I didn't know if I was following anybody's lead or if I was still being led. If the spirit of God was leading me, then his spirit was residing right in my guts. I was driven by gut instinct.

My soul felt raw and exposed, my mind was unrefined. My spirit was willing, but I felt so weak. Once more I held onto my bloodied cross, stripped bare. All I had left to hold onto were my beliefs, my roots that had sewn me together. The year 2011 had come to an end and with it my daughter's death. She took with her my hopes and dreams of a future that will never be. The year 2012 was coming, Charlotte's birthday in February, the anniversary of her death in March, and the launch of something new, a new beginning...

# Chapter 9
## Devote Yourself

In the summer of 1983 it was time to take my final exams at school, my O levels. I was due to take eight exams altogether. I had to change my curriculum in many subjects because of moving from one side of the country to the other. Instead of being under the Oxford Board, I was under the Cambridge Board of Examiners. This proved fatal for my studies as I just couldn't catch up in time for the exams. My geography teacher managed to keep my curriculum the same as I had been studying in Somerset. But when it came to sitting the exam, much to my annoyance, I had been given the wrong paper. I was told quite bluntly that I would have to make do with what I was given.

The unwelcome news just added fuel to the fire of my rebellion. I sat there in the exam hall looking around at everyone scribbling away. All I could do was sit there staring at my geography paper, looking at the topics which I had not studied for. I thought of all the intellectual boffins at Cambridge and Oxford University who put these question papers together. I wondered if the world that they lived in had any relevance to the working world and ordinary people like me. As I pondered these chaotic thoughts, I started to write them down on my paper. I was inspired as I wrote. By the time the exam had ended I had written eleven pages on my opinion of the entire education system and how it was failing people like me.

I felt very proud of my work and finished it off with a bold statement that included four letter expletives. I didn't understand why my whole academic life had to be dependent on my performance in an exam. I wanted a return to apprenticeships, something that was more practical and related to the real working world. Somehow I didn't think that my essay would be very convincing but, like a fool, I handed my anarchic paper in with my exam. I waited for the consequences to unfold and realise the impact of my actions.

My exams were finished and, together with my fellow biker mates, we decided to ride around the school buildings on our last day, revving our engines noisily and throwing eggs at the classroom windows. My maths teacher was literally caught with egg on his face. My last rebellious fling would end with us being chased by the teachers out of the school grounds. Finally, the gates shut firmly behind us. We sped off to the local Queen's Head pub down by the river, where we celebrated our freedom into the night.

It was that night I met Tyler's cousin Steve, a university student who was doing a year's work experience at Marconi's Electronics. Tyler was talking about going to the Stonehenge Rock Festival where Hawkwind were headlining. Steve perked up and said he was going to Greenbelt, a festival where Christian rock bands and Cliff Richard would be performing. We just laughed at him and mocked his Christian faith but I couldn't stop thinking there was something different about this guy.

Coincidently, my mum was reading a book by a Christian writer on the subject of miracles. She was so impressed by the writer that she wrote a letter to him, asking if she could visit him and his family. Surprisingly, she heard from him straight away and was invited to go and stay with his family up in Norwich for the weekend. On her return she behaved like a changed woman, announcing with great enthusiasm that she was now a follower of Jesus. Apparently, he had healed her back trouble that had been bothering her for years. I was glad to see my mum happy for once but sceptical about her new found faith. I just thought it was probably a passing phase, like so many other things in my mother's life.

I continued in my hedonistic pursuits and asked my mum for permission to throw a party at our house. To my delight, she approved and Gerry said he'd go out for the night, so the party was on. My mum, conveniently, spent the evening in her bedroom while we blasted rock music through the house. We drank coke that had rum in it, orange juice which had vodka, and smoked pot in the garden, tripping out to the hippy music. One of my crazy biker mates, nicknamed 'Egg', was smoking something a lot stronger and started hallucinating. He ran into my next door neighbour's garden, punching holes in their lawn, ran back into our garden and collapsed, vomiting on the grass. Then he bolted through the house screaming, "He's coming, he's coming!"

At exactly the same time, Gerry returned home to find Egg kneeling on the front doorstep, mockingly in prayer to some god. This unruly sight infuriated him, and he stormed into the back garden, shouting my name. I was hiding in the dark when suddenly, Gerry slipped on Egg's vomit. Now he was really mad. Looking rather humiliated, Gerry stomped out of the house and drove off in his car. My mum came out of her bedroom and calmly told me to stop the party before Gerry came back to seek revenge. I escorted my friends back to the bus station, merrily singing the night away, before my solemn walk back home.

That was the last time I saw most of my school friends, apart from Tyler. I heard a few weeks later that my friend Egg was killed in a motorbike accident. That night I arrived back home to find Gerry and my mum in the middle of a blazing argument. Gerry was just telling her that he'd had enough of my mum's new religion. She was driving him crazy and he warned us both that we better have locks fitted on our bedroom doors. He said his guide spirit had spoken to him of murder in the night. I thought Gerry had completely lost the plot. The next day I sat my mum down for a good long talk about where she was going with this relationship.

Steve, Tyler's cousin, also came around that day and offered to pray with us. My mum found this comforting and I found myself praying to a god I wasn't even sure I believed in. My mum had decided she wasn't going to confront Gerry any more. Instead she was going to pray that he would pack up and leave of his own accord. Needless to say, my mum and Gerry were sleeping in separate bedrooms. The day after we had prayed together, Gerry fixed a lock on his own bedroom door. I thought how ironic that was and my mum said it was an answer to prayer. I decided to visit Tyler that day but instead Steve was there at his house and I ended up having a long chat with him.

Steve was a tall, slim, fresh faced young academic who was quite out of my league when it came to intellect. I found his conversation stimulating and he seemed to have a strong faith in God. I told him of the conflict going on in my head. I had been reading a literary essay of James Allen, "As a man thinks in his heart, so is he." I asked if he thought a man literally is what he thinks; his character the complete sum of all his thoughts; every action and feeling is preceded by a thought, or are we just a product of our own environment?

Isn't there a destructive force at work in our world that is willing history to repeat itself? Like a mouse running on a wheel in a cage, working hard to reach a destination but never getting there? Isn't this force of life determined to go round in circles? Are we not destined to perpetuate what generations have done before, hell-bent on destruction? Am I not destined to repeat the broken history in my family? Steve and I tossed conversation around for a while until he told me something that was to have a profound impact on my life.

"Forgiveness is the key. It's not the easy way out, like most macho men would have it. Jesus knew that forgiveness was the only way to overcome evil in the world. Forgiveness would empower me and set me free to make clear choices in life and not be a slave to the bitterness and hatred that was eating me up inside. If I wanted to change and not become like the men I despised, I needed to forgive them. This is what would stop my life going round in circles. This is what would stop history repeating itself in my life."

Steve's message resonated deep down to the very core of my inner being, even though it was hard to hear. Before I left

Steve that day he invited me to go to the Greenbelt Festival with him at the weekend. I asked what kind of bands were performing and he mentioned some Christian rock bands that I'd never heard of before. He kept repeating that Cliff Richard was headlining on the Saturday night and that I must come. I wasn't so keen about seeing Cliff but I told him I'd let him know the next day. My journey home seemed longer than usual that night, as I pondered my life's lack of direction.

When I finally reached home, my mum greeted me at the door to tell me that Steve had phoned. He asked if I was okay as I looked 'down and out' when I left him. My mum was also excited to tell me that she would drive Steve and me up to the Greenbelt Festival on Saturday. She wanted to see Cliff Richard too. I said I'd let her know in the morning and shut the door to my bedroom as I wanted to be alone with my thoughts. I knelt down beside my bed, looking up at the night sky through my window. My thoughts were telling me to come to my senses. My heart was telling me I needed some kind of breakthrough.

Then I had an experience that could only be described as supernatural, an epiphany, a spiritual awakening, or a born-again experience. Whatever you may call it I had a personal talk with the Almighty that went something like this:

"Almighty God, if you are really listening, I'm in a bit of a mess here. I've done a good job of screwing my life up and so have others, so I need some help. I want to forgive those who have hurt me. I don't want to let my bitterness determine who I am…"

I paused for a moment as I felt a surge of emotion come over me, an overpowering sense of relief. As if some saviour-like figure had just stood up to the raging storm in my heart and mind to say, "Peace, be still."

This didn't make sense as a few minutes ago I was feeling depressed. I started to laugh and as I laughed I started to cry. Then I just found myself thanking God over and over. I pictured myself kneeling at the foot of the cross that Jesus died on, thanking Him for setting me free and lifting this weight from my soul that I couldn't carry any longer. I had a flashback to the time when I went to see the *Come Together* musical as a child. I felt childlike again, dancing with no inhibitions and not a care in the world.

That was it, my spiritual experience that would always remind me of how far I had come, and the new journey I was embarking on. This journey was not going to include the baggage that was weighing me down before. The path set before me was full of hope and faith for the future. I was enveloped in a sense of euphoria. For the first time I felt I was being given a real purpose in life to fulfill and, with such a strong sense of identity, as if my life depended on it.

Of course, I didn't completely understand all of this spiritual stuff but this experience inspired a new hope within me. It was like I'd been handed a personal mission statement from the Almighty himself. A conviction of truth deep inside, calling me. A truth that would define my purpose in life. I laughed to myself as this reminded me of the movie *The Blues Brothers*. They said they were on a mission from God, except this was not a joke, this was for real. It was dark in my room but I felt no fear; my fear of the dark and nightmares that had haunted me for years were silenced that night.

I still didn't sleep well. I was too excited and couldn't wait to see what was going to happen next. I was enjoying this personal relationship with God and woke the next morning with great expectations. It was Saturday, August 27, 1983 and Steve came over to celebrate and welcome me into my new spiritual family. Then we jumped into my mum's beat-up old Mini and merrily drove off to Greenbelt Festival. The festival was held in the grounds of Knebworth House, a very famous venue for many rock bands like Led Zeppelin.

Greenbelt had an eclectic blend of Christian artists ranging from Jesse Dixon's black gospel to Jerusalem's heavy rock, which impressed me more and definitely strengthened my resolve to play in a rock band like them. Their song 'Constantly Changing' was inspirational in the music and lyrics. When we arrived, the festival was packed with thirty-five thousand people of all ages. As the sun was setting in front of the main stage, Cliff Richard came out to the screams of middle-aged women. Armed with just an acoustic guitar, he led everyone in unison, singing along to his classic hit 'Summer Holiday'.

Yes, even a young punk like me was singing along to Cliff. That was an unforgettable weekend where I forgot about myself, my problems, and lost myself in the music and the moment. It was truly a day spent without my ego.

Before long, it was time for Steve to go back to Bath to finish his degree course at university. I thanked him for everything he had said and done for me over the last few months. I lost touch with Steve over time but I know that whatever he went on to do, he would do it well. He was a good man.

As much as there is an evil force in the world willing history to repeat itself, there is another life-giving force that wants to evolve, to change, to reform, and not conform to the patterns of thought that I had become so accustomed to and felt comfortable with. Truth was not just an 'it', a mysterious force blowing in the wind. The truth is personal and I could find the truth in Jesus. He is the truth that could set me free. This undiscovered belief rises up in me and says enough is enough. I need to change, I want to pack my bags and go on a journey of discovery. For the world I can live in is so much bigger than the world I'm living in right now.

The real battleground was in my own mind and heart, not in the world around me. I couldn't carry on blaming other people for the circumstances of my life. I needed to stand up and be responsible for my own actions. No matter what life had to throw at me or test me with, and because of the free world I live in, I always have a choice of which action to take. I chose the truth and no matter what it takes or costs I was going to follow this truth for the rest of my days. As a new believer in the Christian faith, I had a lot to learn. In fact, I don't think I will ever stop learning about eternal truth.

I really believed God could speak to me personally, not in an audible voice as He did with Moses on the mountain, but in a still small voice somewhere between my heart and my mind. I began to read the Bible every day. I would naively ask God to guide my finger, pointing to a scripture as I opened my Bible. I called it Bible roulette. With great expectation, every scripture my finger was landing on would jump out of the page at me. One morning I opened the Bible to the Book of Joshua, chapter three, verse five. It says, "Devote yourselves, for tomorrow the Lord will do amazing things among you."

These words seemed to burn themselves on my heart as I read them. This became my mission statement as a young Christian. Every day I would pray a prayer of devotion to God and expect Him to do something amazing. I was still having a real battle to be able to sleep at night. I would wake up bathed in sweat, terrified from violent nightmares as I had been for many years. Sometimes I would physically feel as if I was being pinned down on my bed, my chest crushed by an unseen weight and unable to catch my breath. The more I devoted myself to God in prayer, the more intense my nightmares became.

I found help from reading a religious tract about a man who prayed for people's deliverance from the occult and witchcraft. I phoned the contact number and found out that he was part of an organisation called the London Healing Mission. They travelled around different churches with a team holding prayer and healing meetings. I also discovered they were going to lead a service in a church close to where I lived. My mother and I went along and again I felt this great expectation that something amazing was going to happen that night. For eight years I had been plagued with these nightmares and lack of sleep. Now I could finally see a way out of this prison and grasp a new freedom.

We arrived early and were invited to the prayer time before the meeting started. I instantly recognised the man from the tract. His face just seemed to glow. I felt like I was in the presence of some intense aura. I was really nervous, trying not to shake and a frail old man sitting next to me asked very gently if I was afraid. I couldn't speak so I just nodded in affirmation. He reassured me there was no need to be. He laid his hand on my forehead and just spoke a simple prayer for peace. That was it, I immediately stopped shaking and felt a deep calm come over me.

I thought there was going to be a loud prayer of hellfire and brimstone or something. But there was no fanfare, no struggle, and in a matter of seconds I realised I was free from whatever was causing my nightmares. During the worship service the music was very joyful and I watched the old man praying for people. Some would shake like me, some made loud noises, and others would just fall over and then wake up a minute later. For a newcomer like me, this was probably the wackiest church service I'd ever attended.

At the end of the service, which must have carried on for at least two hours, I spoke with this delightful old man. I discovered his name was Jim. He was eighty-six years old and had been doing this kind of thing for the last forty years. He had a very kind-looking face with white hair and a gleeful look in his eyes. I asked him if I could follow him on his healing mission whenever he was near my town. He welcomed the idea and then set off in his old Austin Minor.

When I returned home that night, I was a different person, like a dark shadow had been lifted. I laid in my bed in the darkness and for the first time in eight years I felt calm and still. I slept so peacefully, no nightmares, no fear. I slept so well, I overslept and ended up being late for college the next morning. I could never forget what had happened that night. I loved following Jim around and watching him pray for people. He would not make a big deal about seeing people get healed of all kinds of ailments. He would just quietly and gently pray and sometimes laugh to himself as he witnessed miracle after miracle.

Hanging out with an eighty-six-year-old man wasn't exactly the coolest thing to do for a seventeen-year-old. But I did learn a lot as I observed the way Jim went about doing God's business. He taught me how God loves to surprise us with the things that mean so much, and that if I stay close to Him, I will be surprised too. I loved old Jim. He was a real diamond character, and I was very sad when I learned of his passing away the following year, although I had no doubt I would see him again one day.

At the end of the summer in 1983 I received a very sobering letter from the Cambridge Exam Board. They were rather upset with my anarchic essay on the state of the education system in our country. They were so offended by my words they decided to disqualify all of my O level results. So after spending eleven years of my life inside eleven different schools, I had managed to wreck my educational career.

As a young believer I was learning all about making restitution, putting right the wrongs I had committed against other people. Naturally this involved being humble – not something I was very accustomed to. This meant I had to try and repair the damage I'd done to my education, especially if I wanted to return to college and salvage something from my lost years at school. I resorted to going back to my former school to see if the head teacher could help me out with releasing my O level results. I learned there was a new head teacher and he was my old maths teacher, Mr Smith.

The last time I saw him was when I was riding around the school grounds on my motorbike and threw an egg in his face. Great! Thank you, God. I stood outside his office and tried to prepare myself to be humiliated. As I was waiting, my ex-girlfriend walked past. I couldn't believe she still wanted to flirt with me. The last time I saw her was at a party flirting with some other guy, and I flew into a rage, beating her and the guy with my fists. Restitution was definitely on the agenda that day. I swallowed my pride and apologised to her. She just brushed my apology off with a playful comment about how she likes bad boys. As she walked away, I felt relieved that I was putting my past behind me.

The secretary stepped out and announced that the head teacher was ready to see me. I entered his office in trepidation, walking into unknown territory. I was unfamiliar with this new behaviour of mine and wasn't sure where it would take me. I guess this is what the Bible calls walking by faith and not by sight. Mr Smith's initial reaction to me was guarded. As I continued to explain to him the life-changing event that took place over the summer, he seemed to let down his guard. In my vulnerability, I expressed a heart that was truly sorry for the stupid things I had done at his school. Now with my newfound faith, I was seeking to make amends for the wrongs I had committed.

For a moment there was an awkward silence. Then I felt very emotional about what I had just said. I looked down trying to hide the tears in my eyes. I didn't want to look a fool in front of him. When I looked up, I saw by the expression on Mr Smith's face that he was very moved by my story. With real sincerity he told me that mine was an amazing testimony. He went on to explain that he too was a Christian and a lay minister for the Baptist church. He said that he would try his best to release my O level results from the Cambridge Exam Board and would pray for my success in life and my further education.

I left my old school that day not feeling guilty, bitter or angry like I had done before. I felt like a changed person, relieved of any guilt or bitterness. As hard as it was being transparent about my life, this Christian walk was definitely looking like the best decision I'd ever made. About two weeks later I received an official letter from the Cambridge Exam Board, awarding all of my O level results. Astonishingly I had passed four of the eight O levels. I had already signed up for a BTEC course in Business Studies at the Chelmsford College of Further Education, which at the end of one year would be equivalent to another four O levels.

Now I was starting to see how my faith in God could really change my life. By being open and honest I could make restitution for all the wrongs I had committed. I had to be determined to put my past behind me. This meant leaving behind some of my friends and making new ones. By following through with my commitment, I was changing the course of my life. I couldn't just blag my way through life any more; I had to put my words into action. I was always a dreamer and never had the belief or the assurance to make my dreams come true. Until now. With my faith in God, I felt sure of where I was going and for the first time, I had real hope.

# Chapter 10
## Stranger in a Strange Land

I had come so far in my journey of faith. Remembering the times when I first believed gave me reassurance. Then I could still find a new beginning and realise the dreams of my youth, even after experiencing trauma and sadness in my childhood. After what I'd seen of marriage, I never thought I could be happily married. Marrying Karen was the most natural and easy thing to do. Fatherhood scared the living daylights out of me and yet, raising my own children, giving them the devotion I had never known made me feel rich. I had discovered the Promised Land, put my roots down, and thrived in this place – and then suddenly been ruthlessly kidnapped and transported into a barren wasteland, a desert where nothing was familiar.

My grief has made me feel like a stranger to all of my friends around me. It is as if I have joined some unreached tribe they find difficult to relate to, a language barrier, a culture they find alien. My journey is taking me down a different path, similar to the pilgrim on a journey much less travelled, and a lonely one. Some of my friends are beginning to ask me after almost a year of living without my daughter, "Is it getting better now?"

It's like my grief is some kind of disease or illness that I should be getting over now. But my reality is the pain will never go away; it is a part of my life whether I like it or not. This is the reality and territory I have to familiarize myself with. I am a broken person and always will be. This is grace under pressure and all I can ask for, all I could ever want is more grace.

Karen and I draw great strength from each other by not allowing our grief to stonewall us into living separate lives. Karen lives with regret for letting Charlotte out of the car on that fateful night but she refuses to be frozen in that moment of time. I could blame her for Charlotte's death in order to bring some kind of closure and justification as to why she died. It could be so easy for us to withdraw, stop talking, to stop caring and allow ourselves to be held captive by our grief. Our grief feels like a vacuum of space that cannot be filled, separated by pain.

We choose to knock down the walls that would try to imprison us from each other. We break through the wall of silence and talk, even if it doesn't make any sense. Even if we have nothing to say, we will hold each other's hand to cling onto the love that binds us. I will save my marriage from being broken by emptiness. Karen is the love of my life and worth fighting for.

When our boys need us to help them, we still care about what goes on in their lives. We keep our hope alive by constantly talking with them about Charlotte and helping them practically with things like their homework or time management. We always encourage them to share their feelings, no matter what. I love hanging out with Luke and

Jason. We enjoy each other's company and share so many likes and dislikes. This in turn gives us all strength to carry on.

We choose to reach out and embrace other people's pain to bring comfort. It's the small things that make the real difference, like making a meal or doing the grocery shopping for someone who is going through a hard time. In the same way, some of our friends have reached out and helped us. We still believe that our love for each other can help us walk through the pain of our grief. Karen and I are determined that although our sons have lost their sister, they are not going to lose their parents as well.

Our child psychologist informed us that because of their loss, our boys would find it very difficult to focus on revising and sitting their exams. In order for their brains to compensate for the trauma they were suffering, their visual memory had shut down. This made it incredibly hard for them to remember details. But, due to their sheer determination and the support we gave them, Luke passed all his A level exams with two Bs and a D. Here is how his deputy head teacher at school described his strength of character. "Luke is a calm, sensitively aware young man. His gentle manner belies a steely determination to always give of his best and to see his tasks through. Luke has made a strong circle of friends since joining Charter College in 2009. Luke's care and concern for others has given him the ability to forge strong friendships and positive relationships. Luke made a memorable impression on the young people at our international link school, in the equatorial rainforest in Ashanti-Akim, central Ghana. He worked with great empathy with everyone with whom he came into contact, showing great care and compassion in his dealings with students, staff, and the students' families. He gained a tremendous amount through his participation in this journey. Luke is a determined and committed young person who follows advice and guidance and judges when to ask for support. An example of his determination to succeed, his commitment and his ability to listen carefully to advice and guidance, occurred when Luke demonstrated academic resilience. I believe Luke's overarching 'weakness' to be that he may be considered to be too considerate at times, sometimes to the detriment of himself and his own well-being. An example of this concern for others has been clearly illustrated in a very recent tragic event in which Luke's young sister was killed in a traffic accident. Luke is still in the early stages of mourning her loss but has taken great pains to support his own friends in their shock and her young friends in their distress. He has been extraordinary in his external coping mechanisms at school and has the support of a wonderfully loving and caring family; he has placed other people's needs ahead of his own and may need to take time for himself in the healing process…"

Jason, our second son, was the first to see Charlotte when she was born and the last when she died. On February 9, 1999, at around nine in the morning, Karen was lying in a bed in our lounge in labour. The midwife came around and checked Karen out, she was only three centimetres dilated, and concluded that it would take hours before she was ready to deliver the baby. The midwife said she would come back in an hour to check on how she was doing and promptly left.

About a half an hour later, Karen said she needed to go to the toilet. Fortunately, the toilet was right outside the lounge door, just off the hallway. I was sitting down watching television. Jason, a toddler, was sitting on his potty, his head in both hands. He looked very fed up and humiliated with having to sit down and do his business. We were both watching the classic children's television series *Thunderbirds*. Just before a new episode was about to begin, Karen screamed out, "Neil, I'm having the baby!"

I jumped up and ran into the toilet.

"Quick," Karen said. "It's coming, it's coming!"

I reached into the pan of the toilet, and just as I did, Charlotte slipped out and fell right into my hands. I quickly pulled her out, "It's a girl!" I shouted.

I slapped Charlotte on the bottom to make sure she was breathing. She didn't cry much but just stared serenely into my eyes. I wrapped her in a warm towel and reassured Karen, "We have a beautiful little girl."

"Great, now get me off this toilet!" Karen replied, starting to shake from the shock of giving birth.

Meanwhile, Jason was still watching the television on his potty, five – cue dramatic music – four – three – two – one – Thunderbirds are go! Cue more dramatic music. Charlotte was still attached by her umbilical cord, so I held her closely and, walking backwards, Karen managed to get up. Slowly, in unison with the dramatic and unforgettable *Thunderbirds* music, we walked back to the bed in the lounge. 'FAB Virgil!' I lifted Karen and Charlotte onto the bed and made sure Karen was comfortable. I turned to Jason and said emphatically," Look, Jason! You have a baby sister!"

"Is that yours?" was his nonchalant reply.

Fast forward twelve years and Jason was sitting in the back of the car when Karen was driving Charlotte down the road to her dance lesson. He witnessed his sister running out and being struck by the bus. Seconds later, when the bus stopped, both Karen and Jason leapt out of the car and ran to see if Charlotte was still alive. Jason did a lot of growing up that night and, compassionately holding his mother tightly, he was the protector. Less than three months later he sat and completed four GCSE exams early on in the summertime and, because of his resilience, scored two As and two Bs. This is what his head teacher had to say about him.

"Jason has shown tremendous courage in working through the grief of his sister's death and yet remained focused on his school work. Jason has been instrumental in leading the football mentoring at Falconbrook Primary School, and we have received extremely positive feedback from staff there about the work he and the other boys do. He has been an excellent role model to younger pupils and an asset to the Leadership team as Head of House. Academically, Jason is very capable and just needs to remain calm and focused in his last year at Thames, and he will achieve a very credible set of grades which he can be proud of. Jason is an outstanding young man who I am sure will go onto great things – we wish him well!"

The strength we have together as a family was and is immeasurable. I hope I never underestimate the love a family can give and do not to try and replace it with a cheap substitute. I don't want to numb the pain in a bottle of strong alcohol or look for comfort in the arms of a stranger.

A strong character is not born. It is shaped out of pain and adversity. My father-in-law, Les, knew this all too well when he was a soldier during the Second World War. In 1939 he was part of the British Expeditionary Force retreating back through Belgium to get to Dunkirk in the hope of catching a boat back to England. Just outside of Ypres, his unit came under fire from German mortar shells. His friend was killed in front of him by the blast and he was injured too. He was taken to the hospital in Ypres where his wounds were treated, but he still had an open wound weeping from his backside. The Germans captured him and marched him and thousands of other prisoners of war back to Germany. He remained a prisoner of war until the end in 1945.

Les had two brothers who escaped from Dunkirk and were sent back over to Africa and Italy to fight the Germans in 1942. They were killed in action. That war wound never completely healed in Les' backside and served him as a reminder of his pain and loss. Les' prison camp was liberated by the Americans in 1945. He didn't receive a hero's welcome, no generous discharge from the army, no counselling for being a prisoner of war. He faced a bleak economy back home and with no formal education except what he had learned in the army. He carved out a future for himself, still carrying the pain of his loss.

Les' war and post-war experience made him into a strong character. He became a much-respected civil engineer, a businessman in his local community and president of the local football club, AFC Sudbury. To everyone who knew Les, including myself, our lives were a lot richer for knowing him.

Pain is an alien and enemy to my body. I will try to do everything I can to heal that pain, but there are some wounds that are just too deep and won't heal fully. I have to find a way to live with it and move on. As a young teenager I started to keep fit and work out in a gym. I worked out seven days a week. The rule I learnt back in the day was 'no pain no gain'. The school of life is certainly teaching me the same rule. My pain makes me feel like a stranger in a world where pain can be fixed, and yet I live in an imperfect world full of broken people.

I am looking for an anchor to ground me, to give me hope. My grief makes my emotions unstable and feels like I am treading on shaky ground. The anchor that I need is moving all the time. So how can my faith in God enlighten me about my pain?

Some people have come up to me and said that faith by itself is just another crutch to lean on, another drug to ease the pain. Maybe for some people this is true. For me, my faith has always helped me to face up to the truth about myself and the world I live in. It helps me choose between right and wrong. My faith empowers me to overcome whatever life would throw at me and test the strength of my character and volition. I don't use it so I can run away from the truth or like a drug to help me escape from reality.

Most macho men who have been authority figures in my life would drown themselves in drink or find something to deny their pain. They felt threatened when their strength was lacking and panic when faced with their weaknesses. I can honestly say it is only my faith that keeps me real and the love of my family that has kept me open and honest. I don't want to hide my fears, I want to confront them. With fear, I cannot trust. Only when I choose to walk through the valley in the shadow of my daughter's death can I really know how faith gives me the courage and determination to overcome my fears.

The blunt force of trauma Karen suffered from seeing her own daughter hit and dragged underneath a bus, torn like a rag doll, had fried her brain. For her it felt like a mess of crossed wires, all connected in the wrong places. The trauma had caused her mind to freeze whenever she came to crossing a road, especially in front of a bus. She had to learn how to cross a road all over again to retrain her brain and unravel the trauma. I would cross the road with her arm in arm and gradually she gained the confidence to do it by herself. As you might imagine, this is a very humbling and painful experience for any adult to do.

This is how my family is dealing with the trauma of losing Charlotte. We face it, confront it, because otherwise we would forever be held hostage by the power of fear. If science was true and this world was just a random accident of chaotic energy like Charlotte's death, then this world really is a dark place to live in, without hope or purpose and full of fear. This nihilistic reality is like standing on the edge of a cliff, staring down below into a raging swell of hostile water, willing myself to fall. This tortured thought leads me to the edge of reason, to the end of myself.

It would be so easy for me to fall prey to a bitterroot judgement because my daughter died before her time. This is when most people, so I'm told, lose their faith when tragedies such as mine take place. This begs the question that most of us ask, why does God allow us to suffer if he really cares? When I ask myself this question, I find myself faced with two streams of thought. There is the thought that we can be victorious and not have to suffer sickness or death. We can be healed, witness the miraculous, saved even from death itself.

I too believe in miracles. When my son Luke was just five years old, he was walking with his mum and grandmother to the shops. When they came to cross over a road, there was a zebra crossing that had been neglected and not clearly marked. Luke ran across it and a car didn't see the zebra crossing or Luke and hit him. The impact sent him flying into the air, propelling him twenty or so yards down the road, where he landed on the curb banging his head. Luke stood up straight away, rubbed his head, and cried.

This accident happened right outside Dulwich Hospital where two paramedics witnessed everything. They ran to Luke, put a neck brace around him, and lifted him onto a stretcher. Then together with Karen and his grandmother, they sped off in an ambulance to King's College Hospital only a mile down the road. I was at work and received a phone call from the hospital telling me what had happened and that two policemen were going to pick me up in a squad car. When I arrived at the hospital, I was greeted by Karen and my mother-in-law, Ann, who were smiling and laughing in amazement.

"What's going on?" I asked in astonishment.

"The doctor's just told us that Luke is perfectly all right!" Karen's face was just beaming.

The doctor and the nurses actually looked really annoyed with us, as if we had purposely wasted their valuable time. The car had been travelling at around thirty miles an hour. There was a big dent in the front of the car where it had hit Luke. The way Luke's body had reacted to the impact, by flying through the air, showed that he was hit by some brute force. Despite all that, he suffered only a bump on his head and a scratch on his hip. We had all witnessed a miracle that day and by divine providence Luke had escaped serious injury or possible death.

My second stream of thought is that faith works through suffering. As Mother Teresa famously once said, "You will find Christ in the face of the poor".

Jesus carried a cross of pain and embraced a cross of suffering until his death. In taking up my cross (figuratively speaking) I embrace the process where I have to accept my pain. This keeps me real and dependent on my faith in God. Some wounds never heal properly. I have to work with them and not against them. There is no replacement for Charlotte and I have to carry on without her. My wounds are a reminder of the cross I carry through this life, how far I have come and the journey I'm still on. Jesus died on the cross so that out of his death new life would come.

My grief is my cross and out of the pain of losing my daughter I can bring new life, new hope for other young people like Charlotte. My cross still signifies a place of brokenness. I had spent my entire marriage protecting Karen and my children from the pain of my broken family. My mother was married and divorced four times. For as long as I can remember she had been addicted to valium. I saw how this drug changed her personality over the years, and because of her addiction she never faced the consequences. All the moving around and running away meant she was never properly diagnosed or treated until recently when she was finally diagnosed as schizophrenic.

I lay the blame at the feet of those super rich pharmaceutical companies who don't care about the consequences, and the doctors who are looking for a quick fix for their patients. My mother did eventually break free from her addiction but the damage had already been done. She chose to have nothing to do with me or my family. She never knew Charlotte. I have not seen my mother in sixteen years. I know what it is like to lose a mother and father. Neither of them came to the funeral or even sent a card of condolence.

At least I had no regrets with my children. I have given them everything I could possibly give. I had worked so hard at protecting my family from this kind of brokenness. But there was nothing I could do to stop my boys from the pain of losing their sister. This too broke my heart. I was and still am determined not to let history repeat itself in my family. I have seen too much bitterness from the past take root and grow into a tree of condemnation, isolation and rejection.

All because of hurt and pain in personal relationships, my parents had chosen to judge instead of understand, to condemn instead of forgive, and never to trust again. I will never be able to trust my parents like I did as a child. I could, if I did not choose to forgive, allow that hurt to stop me from trusting anybody else ever again. I would never be able to trust someone openly, deeply and lovingly for the rest of my life. This alone would be tragic. Even so, now, facing the loss of my daughter, I am so tempted to stop caring, to stop reaching out to others, to allow that root of bitterness to take hold in my life and choke the beating heart of love within me.

I know that the day I decide to judge others out of bitterness, to stop loving my neighbour like I love myself, will be the day I lose the battle over my grief and break that sacred trust in a loving God. When I am faced with my deepest, darkest fears, it is in this very place where I find my faith rises up in a Saviour. He floods my inner being with hope. I turn my eyes to a God who still cares and whose heart still breaks with mine. He helps me to face my weaknesses, to embrace my pain. He gives me the strength to carry my cross.

In this realization I find my fear of death has diminished, and I long for the day when I will see my daughter again. A place where there will be no more pain, only pure joy. If my life on Earth is just an audition, then I can't wait to see the prize, my daughter smiling, dancing, in Heaven.

# Chapter 11
## Turning Tragedy into Hope

"It was the worst phone call I've ever received. The usually calm and composed Karen was hysterical and not making any sense. Paul could hear almost every word from the other side of the kitchen and it wasn't even on speakerphone. She pleaded with us to come; there had been an accident. It wasn't clear whether she was hurt or which of the kids were with her but she mentioned something about a bus. Shock ran through my body but I managed to find out where she was. We left the dishes and rushed off, not having a clue what awaited us. All we knew was that something terrible had happened and our friend needed us. Confusion ran through our minds as we tried to make sense of it. Karen called again fifteen minutes later asking where we were, and I asked if she was all right. The reply came."

"No, of course I'm not all right, she's gone."

"It was the first indication that something terrible had happened to Charlotte. We tried to digest this news and prepared ourselves as best as we could for what we'd be walking into. We arrived to the area cordoned off, police cars and officers everywhere, curious bystanders trying to get a peek. The atmosphere was quiet and eerie. We spotted Karen, Luke and Jason standing beside a bus and told the police officer we were friends of theirs. Before he let us though, I asked him how serious it was as I had no clue what had occurred. He pulled us aside and said:

"She didn't make it; you will see the body covered up."

"The words hit me like a bomb. There was no time to digest this news as Karen called us over. I felt sick, helpless and entirely unprepared. Paul held Karen up as her legs buckled and I put my arm around Jason.

Karen turned to me and said, "Heidi, she's right there, she should be with us," she said, as she reached her arms towards Charlotte's covered body.

"I didn't want to look at Charlotte's body or see the shattered windscreen of the bus. Death hung over us. I just couldn't accept that something like this had happened to my second family – that just like that, Charlotte's life was over. I have never felt so helpless in my life. Words seemed foolish, empty and trivial. Luke was hyperventilating, kicking the wall in anger. Jason just stood by composed, comforting his mother. We still didn't know the exact details of what had happened. The police asked us to move away from the bus, so we first sat in a police car for a while and then moved into an ambulance. It was sitting in the ambulance opposite Karen that I was finally able to release my emotions. Tears streamed down my face although I hadn't even started to accept what had happened. Hours later, the ambulance dropped us off at the Leatherbarrow house and the first thing I noticed everywhere were pictures of beautiful Charlotte smiling back at us. When we got home, Paul and I cried and cried long into the night…"

This passage was from our friend, Heidi, and her account of what happened on that dreadful night. It was March 17, 2012. It amazes me how the human mind copes with trauma. I had spent the last year in shock. Only now was my mind and body beginning to wake up to the reality of what had happened, post-traumatic stress. I had lived a whole year without Charlotte probably the most challenging and difficult year of my life. As I looked to the horizon I could see that I still had so far to go, so many more years learning to live without my daughter.

I felt uncomfortable in my own skin. It was like I had climbed the highest mountain only to realise when I reached the peak there was another mountain to climb. I couldn't believe it. It was like living in a parallel universe and I couldn't wait to return to the real world. Except this was the real world in real time. Just when I started to feel I had achieved something, I was hit with the guilt of doing it without Charlotte. This shook me to my very core. I wasn't supposed to be doing this, but I was. I still am.

The simple truth is that no matter how much I want to stop the world and jump off, I can't. Life inexplicably goes on. I have a much heavier weight to carry now. I need as much strength and help as I can get. This is a time when you need your friends to step up and be there for you. This was the time when I found out who my real friends were and I have been both surprised and disappointed. Surprised by those from whom I expected nothing and hurt by some of those from whom I expected more.

This was new territory for me. I was living in a different world and found it hard to know how to judge my expectations of friends. Some of my friends seemed to find it difficult to relate to me and couldn't face our tragedy. On the night of the accident when I was in Germany trying to race back home, I was surprised by a phone call from a friend I had not spoken to for a long time. It must have been very awkward for him but his instinctive reaction when he heard about Charlotte was to call me straight away. He reached out to me when I really needed a friend.

I have been so surprised and moved by friends whom I don't know really well and yet they have wanted to get involved with helping my family and our foundation. They have donated their time, energy and resources to help raise funds for Charlotte's Foundation without any thought of reward for themselves. Some of Karen's friends still continued to deliver meals to our home a year later. This was just one of the many practical ways in which our friends have reached out to us.

I have two friends in particular who have really been there for me. An old friend, who is a professional counsellor, has made time in his busy schedule to meet with me once a month. He has been a lifeline, my safety net. I have known him since I was eighteen years old. He is a wise counsellor and someone to whom I could pour out my heart. Then there was another friend whom I hadn't seen for a couple of years. As soon as he heard about Charlotte, he made contact and has made time for me ever since. He's a good listener, a very intuitive and emotionally intelligent man.

Before our official launch event on the anniversary of Charlotte's death, I had sent out emails to everyone I knew, giving them plenty of time to buy tickets. Unfortunately, some of my friends I had invited were not there:

"Sorry, mate, too busy…"

"I'm working that night…"

Some didn't even bother to respond. I wanted my friends to remember Charlotte, especially at this time. I had given them the perfect opportunity to get involved through the work of the foundation. As a man, I know and understand that I need to be able to do something, to have a project and fix it.

During this first year I had more of a response from complete strangers than I did from some of my own friends. I know that we can't help letting each other down sometimes and I'm sure they were not purposely trying to hurt me. But I wanted so desperately for all of my friends who knew Charlotte to get involved with what we were doing with the foundation in some way. Even though it was so obvious some could not deal with the pain or bear to see us suffering and share it with us.

I looked around and saw my friends moving on with their lives where everything had returned to normal. They were going about their daily routine of taking their daughters to school and their dance classes, celebrating their birthdays, going on holidays together as a whole family, going out for meals and going shopping together. This reality hit me again like a freight train, how these things are so normal and taken for granted. But it isn't, it wasn't, and never will be normal for us.

The truth is that this tragedy had changed us and we were different people now. I'm sure my friends were thinking and talking about Charlotte, but all I wanted was for them to show up. I wanted to see how much they still cared for her. That's a fair statement, isn't it? If I added up what the percentage was of all the people I knew compared to the people I knew who had suffered the loss of a child, it would work out to be less than one percent. I'm convinced the percentages would be the same for most people.

These are exceptional circumstances that surely require an exceptional response? For some of my friends it felt like they had forgotten what had happened only one year ago. Had they forgotten where they were and what they were doing when we lost Charlotte? I'll have to be patient and wait to see how the future unfolds.

I was feeling so sensitive and raw with emotion. I was at a checkpoint. I had a choice to accept the possibility that some of my friends were never going to be able to deal with my loss and this was not their responsibility anyway. I had to realise that this road was a lonely one. This was my own struggle to fight and not for anyone else to bear. This was also a time to move on, to build the work of the foundation with new friends. These were friends who could naturally distance themselves from the pain and did not know my former life but only related to the new. It was time to journey on.

The Half Moon Pub in Putney, South-West London, had just been refurbished. A small and intimate venue steeped in a history of past and present famous artists having graced their stage. This was to be the place where we would launch Charlotte's Foundation on Tuesday, March 20, 2012.

Rumer was our headlining act. She is an Anglo-Pakistani singer and songwriter whose debut album, *Seasons of My Soul*, was released to commercial and critical acclaim in November 2010 through Atlantic Records. The album had already sold over half a million copies in the UK alone and Rumer had been nominated for two Brit Awards (Best British Female, Best British Breakthrough Act). Rumer is a very unassuming person who had first approached us in May 2011 in response to Charlotte's accident. She wrote this letter:

Dear Mr & Mrs Leatherbarrow, I hope you don't mind me writing to you to express my deep condolences for the tragic loss of your beautiful daughter, Charlotte. I live in Herne Hill and was all too aware of the incident as it occurred a hundred yards from my door. For the days and weeks that passed I mourned as I walked past the lamppost as it gathered flowers and tributes, and as tearful young girls accompanied by their solemn parents stood by. As a complete stranger I was so deeply affected by the harrowing incident and I prayed for her family. Now when I see children and their parents walking up the hill it's all I can think about. I wonder how anyone could be so carefree again or any parent could not think about it. I cannot imagine your overwhelming grief. I understand that you have set up a foundation in honour of Charlotte. I enclose a cheque as a humble contribution. But I would like to do more... I am a singer and a songwriter and I perform under the name of Rumer. I would like to perform in honour of Charlotte's memory and to help raise money for your foundation. Do feel free to contact me should a situation arise where you should need a performer, or perhaps we could come up with an idea together. Either way, I just wanted you to know that I would like to help. I think of your family every day because I live so close to where the accident happened. It moves me to think of the pain and suffering you have to endure...Yours Sincerely, Rumer.

Yet again, we were taken by surprise at how generous and kind a complete stranger could be to us. We invited Rumer around to our house for a cup of tea and together we planned the concert in aid of Charlotte's Foundation. Then, almost a year later, here we were actually doing the event. The Half Moon was so supportive, they couldn't do enough for us. They took care of the two hundred and twenty ticket sales that sold out almost immediately and served complimentary food throughout the evening at no expense to us.

"Help us turn our tragedy into hope for other young performers. Help us build a legacy that Charlotte would be proud of."

These were the last words I said on the promotional video that had been projected onto a big screen at the back of the stage. I looked at the faces of different people in the venue, most of whom I didn't know. They looked like they had been moved by what they had seen. Some were overcome with emotion, others looked shocked and some just looked indifferent. Here I was baring my soul for everyone to see, making myself so vulnerable. I thought to myself, I must be crazy. What was I getting into? Even so, my future was emerging out of the greatest pain and becoming so focused, so obvious to me.

I was exposing myself to complete strangers, not really knowing what their reaction would be. I was compelled, inexorably driven to build a future that was not about me. It was about building a legacy for my daughter and making sure her memory lived on. This was the least I could do for her. Most of us get to choose what vocation we do in life, but ever since Charlotte's death I felt mine had been chosen for me. I worked the room that night, talking to people about the foundation and thanking them for coming to the launch. Stephanie, our support act sang a powerful song about hope. Rumer gave a personal tribute to Charlotte and performed so magnanimously.

The Charlotte Leatherbarrow Foundation was set up to help talented eight-to-sixteen year-olds who don't have the means to realise their potential in the performing arts. The aim is to help provide training and support for young performers, both as artists and as individuals so they can flourish in a challenging and competitive world. My emotions were wreaking havoc with my mind. What was I talking about? I had started a new company and my daughter's death was the unique selling point? I must be mad to go around talking about Charlotte all the time to try to persuade people to support her foundation.

Even though I was doing everything I could possibly think of to move on and go forward with my life, my pain would be a constant reminder of what I've lost and how much it was costing me. I felt paralysed. Physically my life was in motion, emotionally I was still standing outside my front door the morning after the accident. I found myself relentlessly digging deep to find a reference of where I had been before and experienced pain. What had I learnt? What kind of strength could I take from my past?

I looked back at the times I lived with my three different father figures and the volatile relationships we had. Every time they knocked me down, I learnt to get back up again. I learnt to fight. I also enjoyed watching the sport of boxing, in particular one of my heroes, Muhammad Ali. For me, what made him one of the all-time greats was not only his lightning punches and quick reflexes but his endurance to take the punches until his opponent became punch-drunk was phenomenal. How many times he was knocked down but still came back and won.

In this fight for the good of my faith, I have probably been knocked down more times than I care to mention. During this last year I really didn't know if I was still able to get back up again but here I was and still am – fighting.

In our first year since forming the foundation we had raised £76,000. Our primary focus was to award scholarships to young performers to help pay for their tuition and training in the performing arts. At first, we didn't receive many applications, which led me to believe that people were still not aware of who we were. So, I decided to get in touch with the *Evening Standard* to see if they would be interested in running a story on Charlotte and her foundation.

They sent over a young reporter to our home to interview us. He was nervous but sincere in his questions. We stressed that we didn't want Charlotte's story just to be known as a tragedy, we wanted it to be one of hope and inspiration. The following week our story went to press, a double-page spread with the title: "We will not be frozen in a moment that we can't change – when the bus hit Charlotte…"

We were pleased with the article. It wasn't too sensationalist and was very genuine. Soon after the story was released I had a phone call from Princess Productions who produced the daytime chat show *Live with Gabby* on Channel Five. Gabby Logan, the presenter, wanted to interview us about Charlotte and her foundation. We had read that Gabby herself had lost her younger brother when she was a teenager and what a devastating effect it had on her family. Her parents divorced soon after losing their son. We thought this was why she was interested in having us on her show.

Turning up at the television studios was a strange experience, sitting in the green room with celebrities. We definitely felt like the odd ones out, being the only non-celebrities. The interview before ours overran so ours was cut short. Gabby was very professional and courteous. At the end of the interview she asked Karen how we were coping as a family. Karen told her how determined we were, and even though we had lost Charlotte, we were not going to let our boys lose their parents too. Gabby was clearly moved by this statement but still managed to finish the interview well and advertise our foundation. We were very grateful for this media coverage, and judging from the social media feedback, lots of people watched the show.

During this time I also decided to put a team together of music industry professionals who were friends of mine. We were going into secondary schools to teach fourteen-to-sixteen year-olds the realities of the music industry, to inform them of the numerous responsibilities within the industry and that it isn't just about being a star. There is also a big media and marketing machine behind every success story. The course was spread out over two days and involved a lot of role play.

We split the class into groups representing different record labels. Next we assigned the key roles within the industry, starting with the president down to the artist and repertoire. The aim was to come up with a summer hit single and the soundest business plan. At the end of the course, each group would give their pitch and showcase their single in front of a panel of professionals who would decide the winner. We called it the CLF Music Industry Course. I chose Charlotte's secondary school to be the first place to roll it out. The school was very welcoming. We had fifty students pre-selected by the school, all very enthusiastic and conscientious during the two days.

The course was a great success both with the students and teachers. This was a very personal experience for me too, working in the same classrooms as Charlotte did when she attended the school. I felt close to her, as if she was standing right next to me the whole time, joining in with the activities. I could see Charlotte enjoying every minute, starting with the icebreaker to the pitching and presenting at the end. This felt so right. I was meant to be making a difference in these young people's lives, giving them something nobody else could bring. This symbolized who Charlotte was and what she gave to the world.

That same month, in June, we sent out a letter to two thousand different performing arts schools, advertising our scholarships to their students. I had a good response, although to begin with only a handful showed real interest in partnering with us. Over the next few months I started to build some good working relationships and with one school in particular called Redroofs. This school is led by a mother whose daughter had died of a rare blood disease when she was just eleven years old. Her sister and her oldest daughter ran the school with her. I found a kindred spirit with these people and liked the way they were so nurturing and caring towards their students.

Redroofs is only a small theatre school but they have already recognised and developed some really good talent. We are now supporting some of these gifted young individuals through our scholarships. A young girl from this school knew and performed with Charlotte in *Billy Elliot*.

Another lady who runs the London Russian Ballet School was very moved by Charlotte's story and got in touch with me. I'm glad she did as I realised we had a similar heart and vision. She has taken on many young people from the local area and developed skills and passion in them to dance. They are taught Russian ballet from the expertise of a former Bolshoi Ballet principal dancer. Some of these young people would probably be on the streets with nothing to do if it wasn't for this school. Sometimes learning to be a ballet dancer can invite ridicule, especially for a boy. But they are so passionate about ballet they are prepared to be mocked by their peers just so they can learn from a master.

These are the real life Billy Elliots, some of whom we are supporting through our scholarships. There is a street dance company where young professionals are coaching underprivileged young people in how to street dance commercially, something I really believe in, and now I'm able to support some of these talented and committed young people. Two of these street dancers knew Charlotte through *Billy Elliot* as well.

Another lady runs Shotton Hall Performing Arts School, from real *Billy Elliot* country in the northeast of England. A young boy called Connor from this school played the part of Michael in the *Billy Elliot* show alongside Charlotte. This is a school brimming with untapped potential and where I will be seeking out more young talent. At the same time I'll be visiting some young event organisers who are busy fundraising for Charlotte's Foundation. They were told about Charlotte's story by their college teacher, whose daughter performs in *Billy Elliot* and knew of her.

All of these stories already written and more yet unwritten will exist because of Charlotte. She has become the common link with everything I do, bringing young people together to help them realise their potential. It was like joining the dots to make a bigger picture of what her foundation was doing. Charlotte's spirit does live on. Even in her death her legacy continues to grow and extends to places where she never even stepped foot. She is with me wherever I go and has already left a lasting impression on people. She is changing young people's lives, she is changing my life, and this is how I am turning my tragedy into hope.

# Chapter 12
## Conviction of Truth

My belief is a conviction of truth, derived from what, exactly? When I was born into this world, I trusted the ones closest to me to tell me the truth and, presumably, live it out for me to imitate. Then at some point I grew up and found out what is true. This didn't always measure up to what I had been taught or conditioned to believe. 'When I was a child, I thought like a child', that the world revolved around me. I was wrong. Some of us still grow up believing this to be true. For me I think I had a wake-up call from an early age.

Belief is a conviction of truth, derived from my own reasoning? My reasoning at the age of eleven was that the truth sucked. I had suffered the consequences of other people's actions which were beyond my control and forged a victim mentality that stayed with me throughout my adolescence. This understanding was founded only on my personal experiences. If I had continued down this path of evaluating truth, it could have been very limiting to grasp any absolute truth about right or wrong.

Could I change my world, change who I am through my own reasoning? Or was I being inexorably drawn towards a destiny that had already been written for me? My reasoning was incomplete and misleading. I wanted to earnestly seek out a new lifestyle not controlled by other people.

Belief is a conviction of truth derived from my own experience? I was on a journey and the road was headed where I could not see the horizon. For some reason my childhood experiences had hit some kind of self-destruct button inside me. I grew up with a chip on my shoulder, a mentality that said, *This world owes me a favour'*. With this kind of thought I was always the underdog, never the champion, always being wronged and persecuted. I was always a slave and never free, always a victim, though if I was honest, it was this victim mentality that was bringing about my own demise. I had to admit that I didn't recognise the grace imparted to me. I still felt like a victim.

I kept my nose clean and stayed out of trouble not because I was reformed. On the contrary, I was waiting to take revenge on those who had hurt me. My view of the world was and is so limited, so unfinished. Even as I write, you are reading only one side of a story. If you were to read everyone else's side, they would paint a bigger picture of what really happened. I seek the truth because I want life to be in high definition. But what I'm left with is a broken and blurred image. What I see is a picture that is out of focus, out of reach, and yet still leaves me wanting more.

Belief is a conviction of truth derived from my own thoughts? Anarchy rules, OK? A contradiction in terms, maybe, and yet this did describe my resolve in a nutshell. The birth of punk in the mid to late seventies was for me a breakaway from the 'modernist' way of thinking, giving way to early post-modernism. No longer did I want to fit into the system as just another cog in the machine. Following truth because it gave me a mass production of the same results was a truth that destroyed any individuality. If I conformed, I would have become a clone living a robotic way of life.

No longer did I want to believe first, before I had experienced what it felt to be a part of something real. I wanted a relationship with truth to see the heart of it and not just to chant it like some monosyllabic magical word.

Belief is a conviction of truth, derived from my own perceptions? In Jewish history whenever there was a significant event that took place, the Jews would always commemorate the occasion. Sometimes they would build an altar or monument to their Hebrew God to thank Him for this moment in time. This would be recorded in the Jewish calendar, celebrated for generations to come as something that changed the course of their history. They would always remember what this event meant to them. These are what I would call defining moments.

I believe we all have defining moments that put a mark in the sand of time. They define who we are and what we will do in life. My decision to follow Christ has certainly defined mine. Is truth just relative or is it absolute? Could what is written in the Bible be the same truth for everyone? There are millions of Christians worldwide who follow the same essential truth about Christianity. God became human and sacrificed His son to save humanity from its own wrong-doing. His son, Jesus, died on a cross and rose again to give us eternal life and a new beginning with His spirit living in us.

Surely this is one of the greatest stories ever told and it has changed so many lives. But the more I believe in the Christian faith, the more differences in beliefs I am faced with and challenged by. As much as the core beliefs unite us, there are other doctrines or principles that divide us too. When I look back on history, these religious divisions have brought so much pain and suffering. My beliefs cannot explain why I am suffering, but they give me a reason to go on living.

Belief is a conviction of truth derived from ancient literature? There is so much talk and criticism of the Bible. How inaccurate it is or whether we can believe its validity at all. Despite this, the Bible still remains one of the world's best sellers, still talked about on television and in movies; so many of its stories have proven to be true. I dared to start following the teachings of Christ. I discovered my whole world was turned upside down. I have committed my life to seeking out His truth.

The more I follow, the more devoted I become. I'm undeniably directed towards a destiny that is so much bigger than me, towards a father's heart that knows me so much better than I know myself. Sometimes I still wake up and look around at the beautiful photographs we have of Charlotte and I don't know if I can live without her. I don't know if I can carry on. The pain is too much to bear. But I cannot and will not censor my story. There is no happy-ever-after to my ending. My faith has to be explicit if I am to face the pain of my loss.

I'm reminded of a man called John Bradford, a Protestant preacher in the sixteenth century, imprisoned in the Tower of London by Mary Tudor. During her short reign as crowned monarch of England, Mary restored the Catholic faith and had over two hundred and eighty religious dissenters burned at the stake. It is recorded that while John Bradford was waiting for his execution, watching other prisoners led to their death, begging for mercy, he said, "There, but for the grace of God, go I."

Even when he was about to be tied to a stake and burned to death, John Bradford was known for being a dignified and gracious man. I don't feel like I'm being led to my execution and certainly not burned at the stake. Nevertheless, I can know what those words really mean as I face my suffering with dignity and grace. Sometimes I feel very alone and my pain isolates me. I look at all my friends around me and none of them have experienced the loss of a child. None of them can really understand. I feel that my grief is my own and belongs to nobody else. This is my fight, my battle, my private war to be lost or won.

On the night that changed my life forever, God allowed my daughter to be taken from this earth. I felt like He had abandoned me. His words fell silent and He left me to face my darkest fears, my worst nightmare. My grief will always remind me of the heavy load I'm carrying on my back and the pain doesn't stop there. It lodges itself in my heart as a constant reminder of what I have lost. I cannot fathom His understanding. Why would He allow me and my family to go through this?

So who am I? I believe I am of intelligent design, created for a good purpose and not a random accident, even though chaos sometimes rules and throws me into the depths of despair. Even there in the darkest place I cannot hide. I see the light of hope. I find the strength to keep on following and I know it is not my own strength. My faith gives me the reason to move on, to become a catalyst for change, not an advocate of chaos, to build up and not to tear down, to bring hope where there is none, to help a new generation to soar on the wings of their potential.

My belief is my conviction of truth. My conviction comes from my journey of faith in a God who cares nonetheless. In this unholy war I call grief, my faith still stands. Even though I have been robbed of a life so precious to me, I will wait patiently and in faith I will rise on the strength of eagles. I will win this war on grief.